This book provides an accessible and nuanced account of school success, distilling significant research and raising important questions about what 'high performance', 'quality teaching' and 'leadership for learning' look like in contemporary times. Essential reading for school and system leaders and those who support them, the book will break open important and generative conversations about teachers' work, student learning, and educational leadership.

Professor Nicole Mockler, *School of Education and Social Work, The University of Sydney, Australia*

This ambitious international volume brings together a range of views and perspectives to challenge school leaders to think again about educational success. It is wide-ranging in scope, covering teaching expertise, leadership, infrastructure, community and equity. It will be a fascinating read for anyone interested in thought-provoking, fresh insights into school reform grounded in research.

Professor Alice Bradbury, *Institute of Education, University College London, UK*

T0383769

Shaping School Success

This book is a unique primer for school professionals, educators and policymakers to develop a solid understanding of the domains essential to cultivating and sustaining successful schools. It also provides essential reading for researchers interested in these issues more broadly.

In response to various sensationalist discourses around schooling that dominate both mainstream and social media, the authors draw upon both long-standing and up-to-date research from around the world to present a more accurate, holistic, and optimistic approach. The book identifies the key domains that are necessary to address concerns in equity, leadership and teaching for enhanced student learning and wellbeing. Specifically, these domains relate to: (1) system-wide approaches to enhance school performance; (2) building teacher capability for student learning; (3) educational leadership as a vehicle for leading learning; and (4) building community 'infrastructures' for equitable, place-based learning. The book can be used in several ways: each chapter can be read as a stand-alone overview of key areas for school improvement. The broad topics are important jigsaw puzzle pieces that are necessary to 'see the whole picture' of a successful school/system. Each chapter includes 'Key messages' and 'Ways forward' and closes with extension questions to further guide thinking through the 'big ideas' presented in each chapter and how they are relevant to different schooling and policy contexts.

Grounded in research into productive and proactive system and school practices from around the world, this book ensures professional educators are equipped with the latest research and practice, without being overwhelmed by the detail.

Ian Hardy is Associate Professor of Education at the School of Education, The University of Queensland, Australia.

Shiralee Poed is Associate Professor at the School of Education, The University of Queensland.

Christina Gowlett is Senior Lecturer at the School of Education, The University of Queensland.

Stephen Heimans is Senior Lecturer at the School of Education, The University of Queensland.

Elizabeth J Edwards is Associate Professor at the School of Education, The University of Queensland.

Danielle Armour is Senior Lecturer, The University of Queensland.

Katherine McLay is Lecturer at the School of Education, The University of Queensland.

Suraiya Abdul Hameed is Lecturer and Program Director of Master Educational Studies in the School of Education, The University of Queensland.

Andrew Beencke recently completed his doctoral thesis at The University of Queensland, focusing on critical thinking education, classroom culture, and virtue epistemology.

Richard Lee is a Global Change Scholar pursuing a doctor of philosophy at the School of Education, The University of Queensland.

Laura Rueda Balaguera is an experienced teaching professional and is currently undertaking her doctoral study at The University of Queensland.

Michelle Ocriciano is a PhD candidate at the School of Education, The University of Queensland.

Shaping School Success
Empowering Educational Leaders

Ian Hardy, Shiralee Poed, Christina Gowlett, Stephen Heimans, Elizabeth J Edwards, Danielle Armour, Katherine McLay, Suraiya Abdul Hameed, Andrew Beencke, Richard Lee, Laura Rueda Balaguera and Michelle Ocriciano

Routledge
Taylor & Francis Group

LONDON AND NEW YORK

Designed cover image: © Getty Images

First published 2025
by Routledge
4 Park Square, Milton Park, Abingdon, Oxon OX14 4RN

and by Routledge
605 Third Avenue, New York, NY 10158

Routledge is an imprint of the Taylor & Francis Group, an informa business

British Library Cataloguing-in-Publication Data
A catalogue record for this book is available from the British Library

ISBN: 978-1-032-66682-2 (hbk)
ISBN: 978-1-032-66681-5 (pbk)
ISBN: 978-1-032-66683-9 (ebk)

DOI: 10.4324/9781032666839

Typeset in Times New Roman
by Apex CoVantage, LLC

Contents

x *Contents*

How to use this book

This book is designed to serve as a primer to support education system and school personnel to develop a holistic sense of the key domains that are necessary to consider when working to foster and sustain successful schools and school systems. It is also relevant to researchers and policymakers interested in educational issues more broadly. The book can be used in several ways:

1. *First, each chapter can be read as a stand-alone overview of key areas for school improvement, specifically:*

   a. *system-wide approaches to enhance school performance;*
   b. *building teacher capability for student learning;*
   c. *educational leadership as a vehicle for leading learning; and*
   d. *building community 'infrastructures' for equitable, place-based learning.*

   Each topic is designed to help schools and policymakers to focus on those areas that are most relevant to them in their professional lives as they strive to enhance their practice.
2. *Secondly, each chapter is sufficiently concise to skim-read the whole volume in one sitting to develop an overarching sense of the most important areas schools and school systems should focus on to enhance their practice. The broad topics are important jigsaw puzzle pieces that are necessary to 'see the whole picture' of a successful school/system.*
3. *Thirdly, the ideas in the book are all grounded in research into effective system and school practices from around the world, and the volume can help you keep up-to-date with the latest research and practice.*

A set of 'key messages' and 'ways forward' throughout each chapter, as well as a set of stimulus questions provided at the end of each chapter, will also assist you to think through how the 'big ideas' presented in each chapter are relevant to *your* schooling and policy context.

We hope you find the book helpful for your professional and academic work and activities and that it will be a comprehensive and useful resource for your ongoing learning.

Author biographies

Ian Hardy is Associate Professor of Education at the School of Education, University of Queensland. Dr Hardy researches and teaches education policy and practice in institutionalised educational settings (schools, universities, vocational education settings).

Shiralee Poed is Associate Professor at the School of Education, University of Queensland, and Chair of the Association for Positive Behaviour Support Australia. Her career spans 35 years and includes working as a teacher/leader in Australian state, Catholic and independent primary, secondary and special schools.

Christina Gowlett is Senior Lecturer at the School of Education, University of Queensland. She uses philosophy and sociology to examine contemporary practices and policies in education. Prior to working at UQ, Christina held a prestigious McKenzie Postdoctoral Research Fellowship at the University of Melbourne. She is an experienced humanities teacher and school leader.

Stephen Heimans is Senior Lecturer at the School of Education, University of Queensland. Dr Heimans is an expert in education policy/leadership enactment, research methodology, and schooling in underserved communities. He is interested in the politics of research and contributes to the study group *International Teacher Education Research Collective*, which explores professionalism, questions of knowledge, and the ethics and politics of teacher education.

Elizabeth J. Edwards is Associate Professor at the School of Education, University of Queensland. Dr Edwards is a registered teacher and psychologist. Her research sits at the intersection of Education and Psychology and examines how wellbeing impacts student success at school.

Danielle Armour is Senior Lecturer at The University of Queensland. She has cultural links to Kamilaroi Country through her paternal lineage. Danielle's research area is in Aboriginal Education and her research focuses on the complexities of working in between Indigenous and Western knowledge systems, particularly in education settings.

Katherine McLay is Lecturer at the School of Education, University of Queensland. She is an expert in initial teacher education practice and policy, with a particular interest in the complexities and challenges of technology-rich teaching and learning contexts. Her research interests include dialogic pedagogy and the identity issues that arise from user engagement with technology.

Suraiya Abdul Hameed is an interdisciplinary leader, educator, and researcher specialising in Educational Leadership at The University of Queensland. She researches in the areas of Educational Leadership, Global Policy and Education, and Equity, Inclusion, Diversity, and Culture. She is currently leading multiple international research projects with international counterparts to improve educational outcomes and to generate networking opportunities with international educators and school leaders.

Andrew Beencke recently completed his Doctoral thesis at The University of Queensland, focusing on critical thinking education, classroom culture, and virtue epistemology. His background as a primary school teacher provides practical insights and direction to his ongoing research.

Richard Lee is a Global Change Scholar pursuing a Doctor of Philosophy through the School of Education, University of Queensland. His research focuses on education governance. Richard aspires to remove barriers to accessing quality public education and to influence public policy so as enable more equitable education systems.

Laura Rueda Balaguera is an experienced teaching professional and is currently undertaking her Doctoral study at The University of Queensland. She is an experienced teaching professional who has found research the best way to understand the complexities of education and transform it positively. As part of her Doctoral journey, she is undertaking a study on datafication practices in schools through multiple educational platforms and their implications for and on school leadership.

Michelle Ocriciano is a PhD candidate and sessional lecturer at The University of Queensland. She possesses over 20 years' expertise in English Language Teaching, spanning initial and continued teacher education. Driven by the question of the purposes of education, her research and teaching are dedicated to respecting and valuing plural epistemologies and ontologies.

1 Introduction

About this book

1.0 Introduction

Students' academic outcomes and socio-emotional wellbeing are framed as the 'keys' to individual future success, the success of nation-states more broadly, and the global community as a whole. This book recognises that within individual countries, there is necessarily a strong focus on such outcomes and wellbeing. However, we also argue that in an increasingly complex social, cultural, economic, and geopolitical environment, we need to take a more comprehensive approach, and think more clearly about how to enhance not only student outcomes/results but the learning and more holistic development of students that underpins, and extends well beyond, such outcomes. This includes taking into account the broader educational ecology in which individual student learning occurs, including systemic reform, the work and learning of teachers, leadership more generally, and the wider educational infrastructure in which such work occurs. Within increasingly complex societies characterised by rapid change in social, economic, political, and environmental conditions, there is a need to not simply advocate for individual outcomes and wellbeing in an abstract sense, but to consider how a broader conception of student learning can be more effectively cultivated – both for enhanced individual flourishing, and the sustainable development of societies more broadly.

While more sensationalist media headlines may decry students' declining standards, portraying schools as rife with disruptive students and bullying behaviours, and in the midst of a mental health 'crisis,' we draw upon both long-standing and up-to-the-minute research to present a more accurate, holistic, and ultimately optimistic approach to productive schooling provision. We seek to provide clear insights into a range of issues relating to school systems, teaching practice, leadership approaches, and the broader infrastructures for learning that are necessary to address concerns about equity. The latter includes adequately recognising the importance of local communities, and place-based approaches.

This book argues that a more holistic conception of learning requires not only changes on the part of individuals and the communities of which they are a part, but also of the schools and school systems that seek to educate the students of today, the citizens of tomorrow, for an ever-changing world. In an increasingly

DOI: 10.4324/9781032666839-1

knowledge-based economy and broader social context characterised by increased uncertainty and precarity, there is a need to take a much more holistic approach to enhancing schools and schooling systems. While more populist and nationalist tendencies have exerted influence in recent times, globalisation processes continue to reconstitute societies, even though this may seem less obvious than in the past. Under such conditions, children in different national settings are portrayed as underperforming compared with their peers; there is a sense in which education is construed as having reached a 'crisis point.' While students in most national settings are reported as lagging behind the highest performing OECD countries, at the same time, average student academic achievement gaps between the highest and lowest students in OECD countries by SES quartile have increased since 2000 and represent approximately three years of learning (Sahlberg, 2021). Given the ubiquity of schooling, examining the evidence base for maximising school performance, as well as trying to reduce such inequities, warrants a closer and more 'global' outlook. Furthermore, with projected increases in psychological problems post-COVID, for example increased anxiety, depression, social challenges, behavioural disorders and reduced academic adjustment amongst adolescents (Branje & Morris, 2021), it is timely to review and develop a more expansive evidence base for maximising the conditions for optimal student learning (and subsequent school performance).

In spite of the sometimes-negative portrayals of schooling, there is also evidence of how successful schools and schooling systems around the world have sought to enhance educational outcomes for their students. Within this broader context of contestation over how best to ensure educational provision, and the need for continued educational reform, the current volume draws on existing literature from around the world, with an emphasis upon four key themes that emerged from a broader review of how to enhance schools and schooling systems. These four themes relate to school performance (understood broadly), teaching expertise, educational leadership, and investment in various kinds of infrastructure designed to address concerns about equity, place, and community. The book provides an overview of each theme, summarises the highlights from the existing reviews of relevant literature, and provides suggestions for further development – including a series of 'key messages' highlighting the primary insights from each chapter (as the chapter unfolds). Alongside these key messages, a set of 'ways forward' are also provided that gesture towards what needs to be done in the future to enhance the success of schools.

Each chapter concludes with a set of overview/extension questions to help the reader consider how important insights derived from the chapter can help inform educational efforts in their own schools and schooling systems. These questions help to focus the reader's understandings related to each of the four themes and important learnings to be derived from existing literature.

1.1 Overview of chapters

The primary foci of each of the four broad domains are outlined here. **Chapter 1** provides an overview of the aims and contents of the book.

Chapter 2 elaborates on system-wide strategies to enhance educational performance, including effective models for reviewing educational performance and providing targeted support for identified needs. This chapter is necessarily wide-ranging, given it attempts to acknowledge a plethora of issues that influence school performance overall and recognise school performance as more than simply an aggregate of individual student performance. Systemic school performance issues relate to understanding school systems as functioning ecologies, the parts of which need to be well understood, and as interacting in conjunction with one another on an ongoing basis. For lower-performing systems, there are also constant pressures to try to shift from 'underperforming' to 'high-performing' status in as short a time as possible. Core foci include an emphasis upon the need for change, constantly developing teachers and associated educators, focusing necessary attention on individual student academic performance to inform teaching approaches, and promoting a culture focused resolutely on student learning. Enhancing academic performance is also a key focus of attention at school system levels. This is a complex phenomenon, however, and requires a more holistic approach to academic data assessment, ensuring attention to data as evidence of learning, and not simply data for data's sake. Teachers' learning is also a key part of system reform and needs to be understood as a career-long undertaking. Systemic reform also necessitates understanding key and increasingly prominent technologies, including generative artificial intelligence. Such technologies are rapidly evolving and provide both affordances and challenges for school and system personnel. Similarly, mobile phone technology is promoted as both a 'solution' and 'problem' to the provision of quality education. Understanding both the affordances and constraints of such technologies enable educators to determine whether and how to employ such technologies in their own contexts.

Chapter 2 also foregrounds issues relating to learning and wellbeing, and how higher-performing systems need to actually account for a broader conception of learning if they are to be successful in their educational endeavours. Holistic education design moves beyond academic performance alone, focusing attention upon the social, emotional, physical, spiritual, and intellectual development of the whole person. Similarly, this shift beyond academic outcomes alone is evident in the need to develop more long-standing understandings of sustainability amongst students, to cultivate a sense of agency amongst students so that they can influence the world in which they live, and to make students realise that broader processes such as climate change are not simply insurmountable problems, beyond the capacity of students to make a substantive and worthwhile contribution. Finally, systemic reform needs to be guided by concerns about equity and how more equitable education can be provided for all students – particularly those who already enter the education system as vulnerable.

Of course, successful educational reform requires consideration of more than broad systemic issues. Chapter 3 focuses on the notion of teaching expertise – impactful teaching and classroom management practices which help enhance educational provision across different demographic cohorts. This includes attention to pedagogical practices that have enhanced students' learning. Teaching expertise also necessitates continued attention to developing capability and building professional knowledge of teachers across their teaching career. It is also necessary to focus attention upon broader systemic levers that are crucial to enhance teacher expertise. This is an example of how this book also seeks to make explicit connections between key foci in different chapters throughout the text as a whole. Teacher expertise also needs to be developed around catering for students with diverse learning needs, including various kinds of abilities and disabilities. It also includes pedagogical practices that are beneficial for Indigenous students more broadly. This includes various kinds of collaborative approaches involving community members working in conjunction with other educators in schools, and culturally responsive approaches more generally.

Chapter 3 also focuses necessary attention on developing capability and building professional knowledge more broadly. This includes initiatives such as coaching models that support ongoing professional learning, in contrast with more traditional stand-alone professional development sessions for teachers. Various systemic levers have also been revealed to help build teacher expertise. These include processes in place to foster instructional/pedagogical coaching and the development of sustainable learning communities. There is also clearly a range of different domains where teachers require additional professional learning; this includes in out-of-field teaching areas and in contexts (such as rural and remote settings) where individual teachers' experience/expertise may be limited.

Chapter 4 elaborates on issues in **educational leadership**, including the need to ensure that conditions under which particular leadership practices are enacted are always taken into account. The chapter begins with an overview of the findings of various meta-studies – large-scale studies of leadership practices found to be consequential for enhancing student learning. However, it also cautions that such studies need to be engaged cautiously for the way in which they can 'strip away' necessary context. The chapter outlines how educational leadership practices should be oriented towards enhancing inclusivity to better ensure more equitable educational provision and outcomes across any given population. Issues of equity and social justice are vital for ensuring educational leadership practices are oriented towards improvement in learning of the most disadvantaged. The chapter also supports what is described as a more globally minded approach to leadership practices; this is particularly important, given how schools and school systems are characterised by increasingly mobile and cosmopolitan populations.

Chapter 4 also flags the importance of managing the administrative requirements of the principalship. The administrative burden of the principalship has increased, and managing its pressures and potentialities is important for sustaining both leaders and those with whom they work and learn. The concern is that as administrative tasks increase, leaders have less energy and time to devote to focus on teaching and, especially, learning. Under these conditions, issues of identity, agency, and autonomy are crucial for developing more sustainable leadership practices. The chapter also flags the importance of supporting flexible rather than more prescriptive approaches to accountability and how more 'authentic' accountabilities are likely to enhance the educational purposes of schooling. Reflecting the sustainability theme in Chapter 2, Chapter 4 also gives attention to forms of responsible leadership that take the non-human world into account.

Chapter 5 focuses on various kinds of **infrastructure investment** – policy settings and approaches that relate to school utilisation disparity and issues of residualisation (concentrations of disadvantage) in the public schooling system that are inadvertently created as a result. The chapter highlights challenges and possibilities associated with infrastructure investment in educational jurisdictions. The chapter commences by focusing on the issue of residualisation – both in terms of concentrations of disadvantaged populations in particular schools, as well as thinking about assets that are available in such schools and which such schools produce. Many efforts to purportedly enhance educational outcomes for students are premised on competitive models of educational provision that pit some communities and their schools against others in the 'race' to improve outcomes. Schools that lack the economic, cultural, and social capital of their peers become sites of relative disadvantage in comparison with neighbouring or other schools in their respective national settings. To help augment the resources and assets available in particular communities, the chapter also advocates for various kinds of 'green infrastructure' as a potential means of cultivating more sustainable communities. Such approaches are also a means of overcoming/responding to environmental/climatic catastrophes (fires, floods, droughts, etc.).

In keeping with the importance of context, Chapter 5 also flags the importance of schools as part of larger 'clusters' or 'precincts' and place-based approaches to pedagogy and schooling more broadly. School-community relations are key to this work. Finally, the chapter emphasises the importance of preparing students for technologically rich futures. This necessitates responding proactively to digital inequity, including considering how schools and communities can work together to support one another to redress digital access shortcomings. Such approaches form part of broader placed-based infrastructures that require various bottom-up approaches to be successful. This includes a range of social pedagogical approaches.

In **Chapter 6**, we conclude the book with a number of cross-theme foci that seek to synthesise across some of the key themes presented in and across each of the chapters. We hope you find this volume helpful as you seek to better understand the complex interplay between school systems, teacher expertise, leadership, and community equity, which are inter-related and contribute towards shaping successful schools and systems.

References

Branje, S., & Morris, A. (2021). The impact of the COVID-19 Pandemic on adolescent emotional, social, and academic adjustment. *Journal of Research on Adolescence*, *31*(3), 486–499.

Sahlberg, P. (2021). *Finnish lessons 3.0: What can the world learn from educational change in Finland?* (3rd ed.). Teachers College Press, Columbia University.

2 A system-wide approach to enhancing education

2.0 Introduction

School systems are perennially seeking to improve organisational processes in an effort to enhance student learning outcomes. At the same time, school systems seek to draw upon a range of metrics and indicators of school and student performance in an effort to capture the effectiveness of educational practices in schools. A range of key indicators are highlighted including, but going beyond, standardised measures of attainment. These relate to student academic growth, engagement and wellbeing, school climate, various general capabilities (including critical and creative thinking), attendance, behaviour, and whether students are categorised as 'at risk.' Attention to clear performance roles and responsibilities, alignment of systems and processes to support performance, the use of differentiated, targeted, and intensive supports, and collaboration between schools at all stages of their performance improvement journeys are all necessary for enhancing education at a system-wide level.

However, these are not the only factors that systems need to take into account. It is also important to understand school and system-wide performance beyond traditional modes of measuring, monitoring, reviewing and planning, particularly in relation to academic outcomes alone. While attention to various metrics can be useful and beneficial, these more traditional measures and metrics exist within a broader learning ecology characterised by efforts to improve system performance as a whole. Within such a system, efforts to enhance student academic performance necessitate improving teachers' learning as a career-long undertaking. (While we mention teachers' learning as a career-long continuum here, we elaborate the importance of teaching and the development of teachers in the following chapter.)

At the same time, considerable effort is expended upon developing educators' understanding and application of educational technologies. Generative Artificial Intelligence (AI), with its emphasis on Large Language Models (LLMs), is rapidly recalibrating what is considered 'authentic' student work. It is also enabling new ways of engaging with students and has the potential to be a tool to enhance differentiation of student learning. However, concerns about the accuracy and efficacy of AI, and a range of integrity issues around its use, also reflect the complexity of integrating such technologies and the ongoing analysis and inquiry they require.

DOI: 10.4324/9781032666839-2

Similarly, mobile phone technologies and the host of apps they enable students to access readily are characterised as simultaneously beneficial and problematic.

These efforts sit alongside recognition of the need to foster a more holistic approach to student learning and wellbeing and ensure education is a force for promoting ecological and social sustainability and for social equity more broadly. This involves moving beyond various deficit approaches to measuring and monitoring school performance according to more traditional academic measures, instead highlighting instances and examples of more successful practice, and the conditions that enable them. While it is important to recognise limitations in these systems, it is also necessary to reveal how various at-risk groups have achieved success.

This chapter presents elaborations of these factors – all revealed as key contributors to enhancing system-wide practices. While there is not an ideal number or specific set of focus areas to prioritise, the literature highlights some important areas within and across different national and international contexts that have led to significant improvements in system-wide educational performance. A synthesis across these studies reveals the following as particularly important areas for consideration:

1. A broad learning ecology;
2. Strategies for moving from low- to high-performing systems;
3. Enhancing academic performance;
4. Teachers' learning as a career-long continuum;
5. Navigating educational technologies;
6. A holistic approach to learning and wellbeing;
7. Educational sustainability; and
8. Fostering equity.

This chapter addresses each of these points in greater detail.

2.1   A broad learning ecology

Student learning does not occur in isolation but within a broader learning 'ecology,' in which system personnel, principals, teachers, and students all interact, engage, and learn in relation to one another. Developing sustained relationships among these actors is essential for the success of the broader learning ecology.

Such interactions are necessary to maximise the use of various forms of data collected about students' learning. Quality management systems within the Local Education Authorities/regions in the Swedish system, for example, are based on three strategies: (1) ensuring data can be used, (2) sustaining leadership at a system level, and (3) promoting ongoing dialogue and engagement between school and system leaders to foster reform (Adolfsson & Håkansson, 2021).

In the first instance, there is a need to foster what is referred to as 'conscious data use' (Adolfsson & Håkansson, 2021) at the system level. Such data use is crucial when different modes of data are used in conjunction with one another to provide a more comprehensive picture of students' attainment. At the same time, this also necessitates selectivity, in order to avoid 'drowning in data':

> Schools collect such an awful lot of data and background information of all kinds. Then they don't know what to do with it.
>
> (Local Education Authority participant in
> Adolfsson & Håkansson, 2021)

To maximise such learnings, effective leadership is vital and must include quality management processes. These processes should ensure clear presentation and delivery of key systemic foci, as well as opportunities for principals to learn from one another in their efforts to deliver on these system requirements. This includes providing opportunities for principals to meet together in various leadership forums, seminars, and other forms of principals' meetings. Enhancing system wide processes also necessitates that those who work at regional/Local Education Authority levels model what they expect from principals in their own interactions with all participants in this ecology.

Various dialogues between principals and education authority/regional managers are also key to enhancing performance and need to focus on school results, various kinds of improvement work, and key features of broader strategic frameworks. Structured discussions that seek to enhance not only school performance but also processes of support within the educational authority/region itself are vital. That is, there is a need for a two-way process of engagement – a genuine dialogue – between all parties involved (Adolfsson & Håkansson, 2021). These dialogue groups could also expand to include assistant principals and teachers assigned specific 'development' projects within their school. Various classroom visits also need to occur as part of this process to gauge the extent to which specific reforms have actually influenced teaching practice and students' learning.

Key message: Successful system change requires understanding school systems as broad ecologies involving ongoing interactions between teachers, principals, and system personnel.

Ways forward: To be most effective, opportunities need to be provided for ongoing dialogue between all members within this broader ecology. Systemic integrity requires functional and effective dialogue between school principals and system personnel in particular, but also between principals so they may learn from one another. Such dialogues need to foreground successful teaching practice and evidence of student learning.

2.2   Strategies for moving from low- to high-performing systems and schools

Crucially, successful systems are organised to foster quality teaching and are underpinned by principles of equity to provide a sustainable infrastructure for learning. This is particularly important for enhancing outcomes in lower-performing schools and systems, given many such schools and systems serve more marginalised communities, and the imperative to ensure all students can access high-quality learning opportunities is greatest in such communities (Darling-Hammond et al., 2017). Such an infrastructure includes teacher involvement in curriculum development at national and state levels, not just at the local/school level. It is also founded on a well-funded and regarded system for the preparation, mentoring, and continuing professional development of teachers.

Research from the United States provides key insights into how school systems can support principals and teachers to enhance the performance of the lowest performing schools in a district Hitt and Meyers (2021). The following areas are flagged as key strategies for moving from low- to high-performing systems: systems leadership, developing and managing talent, building a sustainable instructional/teaching infrastructure, and promoting long-term cultural change.

In relation to **systems leadership**, this entails (1) prioritising change for improvement and communicating its urgency (including clear policies and structures in place to support stakeholders attain goals), (2) monitoring both short- and long-term goals (data, milestones for progress, regular feedback on progress, capitalising on momentum), and (3) customising and targeting support to address teaching and broader organisational needs (including aligning supports with key initiatives and removing other initiatives and responding quickly to needs as they arise).

In relation to **developing and managing talent**, there is a need for: (1) recruiting, developing, retaining, and sustaining capable and responsive teachers and school leaders (including succession planning, in-house development programs, and programs to retain personnel), (2) providing professional learning opportunities (individualised professional learning opportunities, job-embedded coaching, mentoring, and use of high-performing coaches, teachers, and leaders as models and peer coaches), and (3) setting clear performance expectations (explicitly sharing expectations regarding performance, performance management that includes progress monitoring, and capacity to adjust professional learning to attain expectations).

In relation to **building instructional/teaching infrastructure**, it is necessary to: (1) diagnose and respond to student learning needs and using those identified needs to drive teaching decisions (including the use of rapid assessment and adjusting teaching and grouping to students' learning needs), (2) provide rigorous evidence-based instruction/teaching (setting high standards and growth expectations for students, providing supports to ensure evidence is used for planning of teaching, and adjusting plans as gaps in student learning become apparent), and

(3) remove barriers and provide opportunities for students to demonstrate early mastery, including partnering with health, wellness, and youth organisations to develop competencies for success.

Finally, in relation to **shifting the culture**, it is important to: (1) develop a strong culture focused on student learning (celebrating success, developing mastery learning experiences, and providing opportunities for community members to collaborate to explore future possibilities) and (2) solicit and act upon stakeholder input (including gathering and considering overall perceptions, as well as specific stakeholder group perceptions, and acting on constructive feedback). *Appendix A* offers a more detailed account of each of these foci, and a summary of key findings from a literature review on schools that have been successful in moving from low to high performance.

Key message: System change requires attention to a variety of areas: a focus on the need for change, fostering development of teachers and associated educators, focusing on individual student academic performance to inform teaching approaches, and promoting a culture revolving around student learning.

Ways forward: To bring about enhanced system performance, there is a need for more targeted leadership practices (emphasising specific school goals as relevant to the needs of particular school communities), a more systematic approach to teachers' learning across all stages of their careers, and attention to individual student academic performance as well as broader curricular priorities and wellbeing, in a more equitable social context.

2.3   Enhancing academic learning

Several points characterise efforts to enhance academic learning and targeted improvement in schooling settings. Such models are characterised by efforts to do the following:

- Enhance academic performance more broadly;
- Foster a holistic approach to academic data assessment (assessment for learning).

2.3.1   Enhancing academic performance

In relation to *enhancing academic performance*, McAleavy et al. (2018) refer to a variety of factors that have assisted in sustaining success in London schools that were traditionally underperforming. These factors are as follows:

- The quality of leadership in schools and at all levels of the education system;
- The use of data and data literacy as a vehicle to identify productive practice and to challenge underperformance;

- The valuing and use of high-impact professional development for teachers, particularly PD focused on classroom practice and the development of coaching relationships; and
- Ongoing political support and contiguous and coherent policy support over several years.

A key manifestation of these factors is sustained attention to developing relationships between high and low performing schools as a vehicle to enhance performance in the latter. Tapping into the knowledges of the best practitioners in the best schools was referred to as 'school to school knowledge transfer' (McAleavy et al., 2018, p. 23). A key part of this process involved drawing on expertise of expert headteachers to mentor headteachers from schools that were underperforming. To cultivate enhanced learning, data literacy was also fostered amongst 'families of schools' in which schools sought to learn from other schools with similar demographic characteristics but which performed more highly on a range of educational measures. Importantly, the mode of professional development that was supported was one which foregrounded teachers' practice *in situ*, rather than more traditional, externally provided PD. (See next chapter for further elaboration of these points.)

These foci also resonate strongly with various 'drivers of change' theories that have been found to be useful for evaluating educational performance in schools and for challenging underperformance. Sigurðardóttir et al. (2021) drew upon a range of literature in the areas of educational change, leadership studies, analyses of effective professional learning communities and data analyses to come up with a list of key factors to foster enhanced student learning outcomes:

- Coherence in policy from classroom to national level (Fullan & Quinn, 2016);
- Enhancing professional leadership at all levels, aiming at improving classroom practices (Cowan et al., 2012; Fullan, 2016) with a focus on learning (Stoll, 2020);
- Effective use of data, to feed into the improvement process and enhance professional learning (Bernhardt, 2016; Brown & Greany, 2018; Dimmock, 2019; Schildkamp et al., 2017);
- Professional learning at all levels, both formal and informal, consistent with the policy (Boylan & Demack, 2018; Fullan, 2016);
- Building relationships within and between schools (Harris & Jones, 2018; Stoll, 2020).

(Sigurðardóttir et al., 2021, p. 5)

Focusing more closely on issues of teachers' learning as particularly significant for enhancing school performance, Hollweck and Lofthouse (2021) argue that effective *contextual coaching* can serve as an important vehicle for building collaborative professionalism which can in turn lead to school improvement and enhanced student learning outcomes. At its most effective, such coaching is also in keeping with the tenets of collaborative professionalism with their attention to mutual dialogue, joint work, collective responsibility, collaborative inquiry, collective initiative, and the cultivation of collective autonomy (Hargreaves & O'Connor, 2018).

2.3.2 *A holistic approach to academic data assessment*

Much of the attention to *academic data* within models of educational performance is associated with formal and informal assessment. Such modes of assessment serve as key indicators and vehicles for learning. However, within increasingly data-driven systems of education, educational assessment practices have become increasingly divorced from learning, with testing practices and outcomes construed as ends in themselves. This is part of broader processes of the datafication of education and the use of data for educational governance purposes in many school systems around the world (Williamson, 2017). This datafication of education is also enabled by the development of various digital and data infrastructures that foster the generation and collection of large volumes of data and which enable the 'flow' of such data between schools and state education authorities/agencies (Hartong & Förschler, 2019). The emphasis upon various kinds of standardised testing has led to what has been described as the 're-professionalisation' of teaching in which teachers are seen as more amenable to organisational expectations around testing and a residualisation of more 'occupational' concerns about teaching and learning (Brass & Holloway, 2021).

This over-emphasis on data has not gone uncontested, however, with educators, parents, and students resisting the more performative effects of educational assessment processes. Lingard (2021) refers to how standardised testing in the United States has been resisted by groups of parents in New York State where high-stakes testing has been an integral part of the schooling system since President Bush's *No Child Left Behind* (NCLB) was implemented in 2002, which was followed up by President Obama's *Race to the Top* (RTTT) in 2009. Concerns about the USA's poor performance on PISA in 2010 ('2010 PISA shock') led to increased concern about educational attainment in the United States (Lingard, 2021). As a result, the increased attention to testing practices stimulated by NCLB and RTTT continued to exert influence with testing occurring at all grade levels from years 3 to 8. The results from these tests were used for a plethora of school, teacher, and student accountability purposes, resulting in a fetishisation of testing in schools and concerns that emphasis upon high-stakes testing was having adverse effects upon both teaching practice and students' educational experiences.

An evaluation of high-performing education systems in East Asia – specifically Shanghai and Singapore – revealed several important factors to keep in mind for enhanced school and system performance (Reyes & Tan, 2018). Shanghai's and Singapore's performance in international large-scale assessments, particularly PISA, has led to these two cities being regarded as reference societies – sites for policy borrowing and learning by other educational jurisdictions (Steiner-Khamsi, 2022). However, within such systems, there is recognition of the need to adopt more *holistic approaches to assessment for learning* rather than becoming fixated on various external measures of attainment. These more holistic approaches involve capturing more complex aspects of student achievement than segmented knowledges (Pellegrino et al., 2001). At the same time, there is a need to implement more assessment for learning practices (Shepard, 2000).

2.3.2.1 *The case of Shanghai*

In spite of success on PISA in recent years, Shanghai has affirmed that its current education situation is not ideal and is in need of change. Arguably, Shanghai possesses an 'exam-driven, time-consuming, and stressful education system' resulting in 'widespread public dissatisfaction with the local education model for the past few decades' (Tan & Reyes, 2018, p. 67). Reform of *gaokao*/high-stakes examinations champions broad-based learning and directs higher education institutions to take a more comprehensive approach towards student admissions. Under this assessment reform, students are evaluated on their performance of real-life tasks through experiments, oral presentations, poster displays, and research projects (Shen, 2007; Tan, 2013). The new 'integrated quality appraisal' system (*zonghe suzhi pingjia*) evaluates individual students on not only subjects taken and academic results achieved but also on capacity to innovate, practical abilities, physical and mental health, interests, character development, as well as more culturally specific foci, such as understandings of traditional Chinese culture. Unlike summative exams, integrated quality appraisal is formative as it accumulates evidence of the daily and more well-rounded growth and achievement of students throughout their learning years. Using *both quantitative and qualitative measurements*, this appraisal system enables students to understand their own strengths and areas of improvement including in relation to ethics, citizenship capacities, learning ability, social interaction and cooperation, and participation in sports, health, and aesthetics.

2.3.2.2 *The case of Singapore*

Singapore has recognised the need to constantly reform, given it faces a complex and uncertain future; its precarity drives continual striving to enhance the quality of its educational provision (Hardy et al., 2020). Arguably, Singapore has 'embraced the goal of achieving new economic competencies dealing with creativity and innovation while clinging to high-stakes testing as the prime yardstick of meritocracy' (Reyes & Gopinathan, 2015, p. 152). However, in keeping with efforts to ensure a more holistic approach to education provision, Singapore has more recently sought to broaden its attention beyond academic measures alone. There has been much greater attention to developing thinking skills and nurturing the spirit and values required for Singaporeans to thrive in a *more globalised, innovation-driven future*, even as it is recognised that much more work needs to be done in this area (Ng, 2017; M. Wong et al., 2021). This involves valuing students' holistic development of competencies, such as critical thinking, innovation and creativity, communication, collaboration, independent learning, lifelong learning, information and communication technology, and active citizenship. Many of these soft skills involve ongoing learning processes and cannot be assessed by one-shot, traditional standardised paper-and-pen tests; instead, formative, authentic, and school-based assessments are required and have become viable alternatives (Koh & Luke, 2009). Rather than assessment for purposes of 'sifting and sorting,' there is now a shift towards assessment as a vehicle to enhance student learning (Tan, 2022).

Key message: Effective models for evaluating educational performance at school- and system-level need to consider academic performance data but also the extent to which assessment is undertaken for learning (rather than for the sake of collecting assessment data).

Ways forward: Any review of educational performance needs to take into account a more holistic approach to academic performance data, ensuring not only improvement in learning outcomes (via high-impact PD and leadership practices) but also what such outcomes indicate about students' actual learning and development more broadly. There is a need for assessment for learning, which helps foster creativity, and to ensure such learning is evident across the whole population (equity) and resulting in students' individual confidence to face the world (wellbeing).

2.4 Teachers' learning as a career-long continuum

Another key theme within the literature is how to foster enhanced teacher practice at a systemic level across the teaching career. Darling-Hammond et al. (2017) refer to a number of practices that have characterised policy borrowing and 'learning from success' of high-performing jurisdictions. The foci of such practices have included the following:

- The use of professional standards to guide teaching practice;
- The development of teacher registration and certification systems to ascertain teachers' competence to enter the profession and for advancement in the profession;
- Designs for teacher preparation focused on clinical practice;
- Professional development strategies such as lesson study and action research (Darling-Hammond et al., 2017, p. 214).

Within teacher education, there have also been calls for increased attention to *developing teachers' capacities to be responsive to unpredictable challenges*, such as the COVID-19 pandemic. There has also been support for the development of various 'hybrid spaces' to enable universities, schools, and communities to interact to develop a broader knowledge base to inform teacher development (Mayer et al., 2017). This also demands increased attention to professional excellence, greater ethical responsibility, and a more innovative mindset within all facets of teacher education (Tang & Cheng, 2021; see *Appendix B* for an elaboration of these points). Teacher buoyancy – the capacity to respond proactively to the everyday challenges of teaching and not to become overwhelmed – is also key to sustainable career development (A.K. Wong et al., 2021).

Various kinds of lesson study (originating in Asia) and action research have also been associated with successful educational systems. As Darling-Hammond et al. (2017) argue:

> Traditional lesson study and other forms of teacher action research . . . engage teachers in looking at practice with a critical eye, often in collaboration with others, to test and evaluate which strategies are most successful for students. Action research takes several forms, but similar to lesson study, it involves teachers jointly conducting observation and examination of a practice, analyzing and interpreting findings, and proposing and enacting strategies for improvement.
>
> (p. 223)

This spectrum of learning begins with pre-service teacher education. Key learnings from what are considered high-performing schooling systems have focused on: (1) a high regard for the teaching profession, (2) selectivity into the profession, (3) financial support to assist with preparation and professional learning, (4) clear delineation of professional standards, and (5) attention to well-defined curriculum content and practicum experience in schools (Darling-Hammond et al., 2017; Sahlberg, 2021). Such a spectrum begins with undergraduate Initial Teacher Education (ITE) programs and feeds into continuing professional learning, with attention to: (1) teaching as a research-informed and engaged profession; (2) teaching as a collaborative enterprise rather than an individual undertaking, including in relation to planning and assessment (moderation); and (3) opportunities for leadership at school and system levels (Darling-Hammond et al., 2017). *Appendix C* provides a list of ten key themes delineated to help support system change based on quality teaching for every child across a continuum from ITE through to continuing teacher development.

Lastly, it is also important to note the intricate interplay between teachers' learning, student outcomes, and the broader social context. Research has revealed that teachers account for approximately 10–15% of the variability in students' test scores; home background/social circumstances account for much greater variability (Sahlberg, 2020). Consequently, issues of equity in education need to be considered alongside teachers' learning to have real benefits.

Key message: Enhancing teacher professional practice at a systemic level is critical to student success.

Ways forward: Education systems need to draw on practices from high-performing schools and regions, emphasising the use of professional standards, teacher registration and certification systems, evidence-informed teacher preparation, and professional development strategies like lesson study and action research, with an overarching focus on continuous learning, responsiveness to challenges, and the interplay between teachers' learning, student outcomes, and the broader social context.

2.5 Navigating new frontiers through educational technology

2.5.1 *Generative artificial intelligence*

Generative artificial intelligence (AI) is proving to be a transformational technology. Much of the debate around generative AI is focused on whether schools, teachers, and students should use these technologies and how these technologies should be deployed in ethical and educative ways. In a think-piece about generative AI, Stefania Giannini (2023), Assistant Director-General for Education at UNESCO, describes how such technologies enable a mimetic approach to language which has not been previously possible. This has significant implications for education:

> We are coming to understand that our monopoly on advanced language – a natural ability, cultivated through education, and our species' most defining social trait – is no longer something we can take for granted. Recognizing this fact is forcing us to revisit the beliefs and assumptions that uphold our current education systems and, indeed, our wider societies.
>
> (Giannini, 2023, p. 2)

This is a challenging situation, given leading technology experts do not themselves fully understand the implications of rapid advancements in AI, including unanticipated effects. Research reveals both benefits and challenges associated with AI use of large language models (LLMs) to generate content.

Reviews of relevant literature reveal a number of potential benefits with generative AI, including the following:

- As an evaluation tool to assess student work (for formative and potentially summative purposes), particularly standardised assessments;
- Reducing teacher workload so as to enable more individual mentoring and coaching of students;
- Individual tuition of students;
- Development of more interactive pedagogical practices as part of classroom teaching practices;
- Development of lesson plans and related resources.

However, at the same time, generative AI also present a number of challenges:

- Generation of a sense of uncertainty about the future, including potential job losses;
- Concerns about accuracy and reliability of generated material;
- Concerns about inherent biases within the data sets upon which LLM algorithms are trained;
- Inability to discriminate between the range of sources drawn upon to generate texts;

- Difficulty of evaluating the quality of student work and to discern students' actual understanding of topics;
- Concerns about lack of fairness between students who have accessed generative AI and those who have not;
- Concerns about data privacy and security concerns (Grassini, 2023).

Some of the concerns that have attracted the most attention have been around the accuracy and reliability of such technologies, given the unfiltered data sets upon which various algorithms have been developed serve as the 'raw material' from which AI draws to generate various texts. Unintended biases invariably filter into the texts and other resources generated through such models. Furthermore, concerns about plagiarism are increasingly prevalent, even as various plagiarism software is constantly evolving (Grassini, 2023). Additionally, the generation of outright false and misleading information has been recognised as a major concern (Gravel et al., 2023), which can only be addressed via constant critical analyses of sources.

In spite of the uncertainty surrounding LLMs and various modes of generative AI, it is clearly apparent that students (at all levels) require critical capacities and dispositions to evaluate the trustworthiness, efficacy and value of artificially generated materials. Such capacities and dispositions cannot themselves be 'artificially generated' but instead are the result of careful engagement between students and teachers about the nature of artificially generated texts and other resources.

2.5.2   Mobile phones and smartphones

Mobile phones and particularly smartphones have numerous characteristics making them attractive to children and adolescents and are fast becoming integral to their social lives. Adolescence is a critical period for socialising between peers with young people reporting a heightened need to be socially accepted. As such, some research has suggested that mobile and smartphone usage is a coping mechanism for stressors of daily life (Kuss et al., 2018). Other studies have shown support for incorporating mobile technology, including mobile phones, in the classroom to supplement learning and support student collaboration (Ferreira et al., 2018). However, a plethora of research has linked excessive mobile phone use or problem smartphone use to lower self-esteem, elevated social anxiety, stress and depression, poor sleep, and addictive-like behaviours such as nomophobia ('no-mobile-phobia') (Edwards et al., 2022).

While most students communicate and learn through mobile technology, many adults have wrongly labelled the current generation as *digital natives* (Goldsmith, 2014). Although students may be very competent at searching the internet, communicating effectively on social media, and switching effortlessly between applications, they also report being overwhelmed by information and can struggle with digital mastery (Neumann, 2016). Thus, despite support for the use of mobile technology in education (Kessel et al., 2020), the last two decades has seen an increasing number of schools and education departments (or jurisdictions), choosing to ban mobile phones.

The introduction of the first smartphone in 2007 sparked the onset of mobile phone restrictions and bans across the globe, for example, US states (2008–2012; many now reversed), India (2005; reinforced in 2019), Japan (2009; reversed in 2019), France (2017), China's Shandong province (2018), Canada's Ontario (2019), and most Australian states (from 2022). Other countries, such as Denmark, Sweden, Chile, England, Wales, and Spain, are considering similar restrictions (Selwyn & Aagaard, 2021).

Mobile phone bans adopt the stance that policies are 'keep[ing] children safe from technology' (Orlando, 2019, p. 8) and the view that mobile phones are a distraction to learning (Kates et al., 2018). However, Selwyn and Aagaard (2021) argue that the impetus for mobile phone policies in schools are often championed by politicians responding to community concerns which are amplified by the media and have limited empirical evidence. As a result,

> [t]here is now an emerging worldwide trend for mobile phones being banned from classrooms and schools. While some academics working in the area of educational technology have raised concerns, many others have so far failed to respond to what is a significant shift in the ongoing development of digital education.
>
> (Selwyn & Aagaard, 2021, p. 8)

A scoping review of the literature for and against mobile phone bans in schools was conducted by Campbell and Edwards (2024) to address whether mobile phones at school impact students' academic outcomes (learning, distractibility, cheating), mental health and wellbeing, and incidence rates of bullying/cyberbullying. Campbell and Edwards identified 22 studies that examined the benefits (for) and/or harm (against) mobile phone use in schools. These studies were conducted in 12 countries (Bermuda, China, Czech Republic, Ghana, Malawi, Norway, South Africa, Spain, Sweden, Thailand, the UK, the USA). While Campbell and Edwards found no randomised controlled trials, they synthesised evidence from studies with different designs, samples, mobile phone restrictions (i.e. partial, or complete bans), and outcome measures. Despite some challenges related to the heterogeneity of the methods used across studies, the following benefits of mobile phone bans were noted:

- Four studies claimed direct positive effects of mobile phone bans on academic outcomes. However, two studies did not differentiate between partial and complete mobile phone bans such that some students were able to use their phones for learning purposes, and two other studies only noted improved academic outcomes in disadvantaged or low-achieving students.
- Two studies reported that mobile phone bans had positive effects on students' mental health; however, these findings were merely teachers' and parents'

perceptions. Two other quasi-experimental studies showed no differences in psychological wellbeing following mobile phone bans.
• Four studies found a small reduction (pre-post) in bullying incidents in schools that imposed mobile phone bans especially in older students. Two other studies found that educators believed that mobile phones in schools facilitate cyberbullying.

On the other hand, the following harms of mobile phone bans were reported:

• Three studies reported no differences in academic outcomes regardless of mobile phone bans. Two of these studies used large samples (e.g. 30% of all schools in Norway and an entire cohort in Sweden) and one study manipulated mobile phone availability in a quasi-experimental design. Methodological strengths suggested results to be reliable and generalisable.
• Three studies reported negative associations between mobile phone bans and students' mental health and wellbeing. Two studies indicated students' perceptions were that they felt more anxious without access to their mobile phone and one study suggested this was particularly evident returning to face-to-face classes following the pandemic.
• Two studies showed that incidents of online victimisation and harassment were greater in schools with mobile phone bans compared to schools without bans.

Taken together, the studies identified in Campbell and Edwards (2024) review suggest that evidence for mobile phone bans improving academic outcomes, protecting students mental health and wellbeing, and reducing rates of bullying/cyberbullying, is not clear-cut. For academic outcomes, that mobile phone bans contribute to improved academic outcomes was restricted to students from disadvantaged backgrounds or those already struggling academically. However, there may be a range of other attributes influencing students from low socioeconomic backgrounds or those with learning difficulties that may have also contributed to the findings; some students may be more impulsive and/or distractible more generally and therefore more vulnerable to the presence of mobile phones in the classroom. For mental health and wellbeing, the findings were inconclusive and based on anecdotes or perceptions rather than recorded incidences of mental illness. For bullying/cyberbullying, the findings were divided. It is important to consider that banning mobile phones and not banning other internet-enabled devices in schools is a simplistic solution. That is, students can use laptops, tablets, smartwatches, or library computers to conduct cyberbullying. Furthermore, cyberbullying may start at school but continue online after school. Therefore, banning mobile phones also has the risk of driving bullying behaviour underground or making those engaged in it more devious in their activities (Brewer, 2014). Campbell and Edwards (2024) suggested that more rigorous investigations of the effects of mobile phone usage in schools is needed before deciding conclusively for or against mobile phone bans in schools. Further, they suggest the solution rests with teaching students critical digital mastery and responsible device use in schools.

> **Key message**: Navigating new technologies in education poses challenges related to adapting to rapid advancements, ensuring equitable access, and effectively integrating innovative tools into pedagogical practices.
>
> **Ways forward**: Schools are uniquely placed to teach students about the safe practices of using new technologies with professionalism and integrity. Educators need to ensure students develop both digital mastery and responsible use of current and emerging technologies as part of school curricula.

2.6   A holistic approach to learning and wellbeing

Recent research has advocated a more holistic approach to learning, beyond various kinds of academic performance indicators, in particular. Lee et al. (2014) compared two high-performing education systems, Finland and Singapore, which infused holistic education into their cultural practices that were crucial to society more broadly. The study posited the importance of extending notions of student agency, respect, dignity, and care as a means of cultivating student wellbeing within the societies in which they lived and learned. Students were recognised as stakeholders of wider social networks, and their educational experiences were an important part of productive recursive relationships between education and broader society. Similarly, Caine and Caine (2010) emphasised the social nature of learning, as demonstrated in fields across psychology, sociology, and organisational development. Tan (2018) elaborated what she described as the 'East Asian Educational Model (EAEM)' to reflect upon the key foci that characterise high-performing education systems. Such a model is influenced by a more holistic approach, including the following:

- A variety of worldviews and dispositions;
- A focus on attaining high performance, which also involves balancing academic excellence and more holistic development;
- Attention to processes of educational harmonisation, which involve seeking to engage productively with complex and often contradictory aims to attain desired educational outcomes.

Despite a reputation for undue attention to examination processes and outcomes, the three contexts to which Tan (2018) refers – Singapore, Shanghai, and Hong Kong – have increasingly sought to challenge more limited focus on results alone and to promote processes of 'educational harmonisation.' This includes fostering both breadth and depth in curriculum, teacher-directed as well as student-engaged approaches, engaging in assessment of learning and assessment for learning, and fostering processes of both centralisation and decentralisation (respecting local processes towards the attainment of common educational goals/standards).

As part of this more holistic approach, there is also increased attention to issues of wellbeing. Drawing on literature from a recent report on the wellbeing of Australian children (Noble et al., 2021), it is apparent that the *implications of COVID-19 and climate change for schools* are important. Biddle et al. (2021) investigated the effect of COVID-19 on the wellbeing of Australian children. They reported that compared to before the pandemic, young people had lower satisfaction with life, worse mental health, and lower confidence in achieving their future career goals. It is likely that given the impact on employment post-pandemic and the association between parental employment and youth mental health, COVID-19 will likely have downstream implications for potential employability and income of young people into the future (Borland & Charlton, 2020). (See also *Appendix D* for details about 'The Nest' initiative from the Australian Research Alliance for Children and Youth (ARACY) with its focus on a range of interconnected domains to promote student wellbeing.)

COVID-19 saw a shift to online learning that has benefitted some children (Gore et al., 2021) yet widened an already inequitable educational gap for children who experience vulnerability. For example, some socio-economically disadvantaged children as well as some living in rural and remote areas were unable to access digitalised learning; for these learners, significant catching up is required (Noble et al., 2021). Noble and colleagues (2021) argue that policy responses should be centred on effective catch-up programs to reduce this inequity.

In relation to students' needs more broadly, but also other members of the learning community, Balica (2020) presents an 'integrated wellbeing approach' summary to support and promote wellbeing in the school community. This integrated wellbeing approach supports students, educators and community members' unique journeys to foster a more peaceful learning environment. Balica (2020) promoted five key approaches to foster wellbeing. These include the importance of learning from crises, becoming more comfortable with uncertainty, investing in routines to foster wellbeing, redesigning and reworking wellbeing pedagogies, and being willing to experiment, share, and innovate. Each of these are outlined in more detail here:

- **Learn from the crisis.** It is important to recognise the opportunities for learning and development that can arise during and after a crisis. By reflecting on past actions and considering what works well and what needs to be changed, there are opportunities to turn a time of crisis into a unique learning experience to reflect on past actions.
- **Become comfortable with uncertainty.** Accept that uncertainty is the 'new normal.' Embracing uncertainty, strengthening relationships, and creating safer learning environments are valuable ways to enhance student, teacher, and community wellbeing. It is important to approach complexity and crisis with forethought and determination to strengthen resourcefulness and resilience in the face of challenges and change.
- **Invest time in wellbeing routines.** Investing time in wellbeing routines is crucial, especially during times of crisis. It is important to prioritise the wellbeing of all members of the school community and create a safe and trusting learning environment. This can be achieved by monitoring the wellbeing of members of

the learning community and implementing new routines that promote support strategies to deal with challenges. The learning community can develop a sense of belonging and resilience through strengthened relationships and embedding wellbeing practices into daily school experiences.

- **Redesign a wellbeing pedagogy.** Use the crisis as an opportunity to redesign a wellbeing pedagogy that encourages the learning community to overcome adversity and to overcome distress. Redesigning a wellbeing pedagogy involves encouraging students to set individual goals and incorporate wellbeing practices into daily school experience. This redesigning process also entails incorporating learning activities that strengthen relationships and collaborative work, fostering a sense of belonging to the school community during times of disruption. By redesigning wellbeing pedagogies, schools can prioritise holistic development and wellbeing, creating a safe and supportive learning environment. Additionally, it is essential to mindfully plan school activities and workloads to prevent overwhelming demands on students, teachers, and the wider community.
- **Dare to experiment, share, and innovate.** It is important to trust the learning community's capacity to experiment, share, learn, and innovate in specific contexts. UNESCO (2020) emphasises the need for innovative approaches to ensure continuous learning and to address the emotional wellbeing of students during these disruptions. Daring to experiment, share, and innovate within specific contexts is essential for navigating through challenging times and reflecting on past actions.

Drawing upon the Sustainable Happiness Project, Alam (2022) discusses the concept of 'sustainable happiness' and its potential impact on education and society. He highlights the need for a shift in mindset and behaviour towards a more environmentally friendly future, recognising the negative effects of technology on individuals' lives and promoting activities that foster happiness and wellbeing, such as spending time with loved ones and engaging in environmentally friendly practices. Both formal and non-formal education should play a role in increasing public knowledge and stimulating creative thinking. However, the current educational system may not be prepared to meet this challenge and there is a need for a transformation in education to prioritise long-term contentment and sustainable wellbeing (Alam, 2022).

Key message: Holistic education design seeks to move beyond academic performance indicators alone and instead focus also upon the social, emotional, physical, spiritual, and intellectual development of the whole person. A holistic education encourages students and the broader learning community to interact with knowledge in a relational manner, in order to achieve optimal functioning, agency, and wellbeing.

Ways forward: Schools and teachers are most successful when they integrate a wellbeing approach into teaching practice that assists students in cultivating healthy and functional relationships with themselves and their community.

2.7   Educational sustainability

Issues of sustainability have become increasingly important over time with recognition that human activity has posed a significant threat to the broader environment (Simmons & Sanders, 2022). This is most evident in relation to climate change. Alam (2022) suggests that incorporating such topics into education can help students understand how their consumption choices impact their overall wellbeing and the environment. Such work involves cultivating both student agency, as well as fostering a more societist approach/ethics which seeks to encourage collective responsibility.

2.7.1   Agency: recognising and valuing students' perspectives

> Our emphasis is on the young as agents, not as recipients or objects of education.
> (Kiilakoski & Piispa, 2023, p. 211)

For over a decade, climate change experts have been encouraging change. This includes fostering healthy intergenerational conversations about environmental sustainability. Kemmis and Mahon (2023) highlight the role of agency in human development and the co-constitution of people and the world and advocate for a transformative view that goes beyond reacting or responding to existing conditions and instead actively co-creates alternative ways of being. This is consistent with Biesta's (2021) call for a fundamental shift in how the purposes of education should be conceptualised as 'meeting' the world.

In this process of 'meeting' the world, young people offer important knowledge, ideas, and activism to help find solutions and hold policymakers to account. This is the case, even though they are often overlooked. Indeed, Kiilakoski and Piispa (2023) argue that '[a]lthough it might be a common conception that young people are the future, they are often downplayed and not accepted as full participants in political debates and decision-making about the future' (p. 211). Educators have a responsibility to cultivate and listen deeply to the voices of future generations, and address their disenfranchisement in shaping the future (Kemmis & Mahon, 2023).

To help redress this situation, schools are places that can help to foster these early discussions in a safe and supportive environment (Noble et al., 2021). Students actively learn in these settings, at the same time as they are exposed to a multitude of learnings within the wider environments in which they live. On such a rendering, all of these learning environments (both virtual and physical spaces) need to be understood as sites of learning in which students can and should be encouraged to engage and develop considered positions about challenging issues.

Students and young people can be empowered through their participation in social movements, which provide a valuable ecology to support the development of student and community agency, and understanding of broader social issues. Within such agentic communities, Kiilakoski and Piispa (2023) suggest the need for the intellectual heritage of democratic principles to be constantly preserved, cultivated, and renewed. Considering social movements often articulate common concerns, it is important to encourage a democratic ethos that fosters active participation through education for democracy (Biesta, 2011). In this instance, such active participation requires promoting interconnectedness of the ecological and the social to enable equitable modes of governance and citizenship that produce meaningful engagements with democracy (Kiilakoski & Piispa, 2023). Social movements such as those associated with climate change necessitate active citizenship within the community for sustainable development. Education for democracy should be imbued with routines and learning experiences that develop young people and their communities, helping these communities to forge social movements for sustainable change within existing and future political conditions.

2.7.2   *A collective ethics: beyond the individual*

These notions of agency are not simply individual, but also collective. When the United Nations Conference of the Parties (COP 26) on Climate Change in November 2021 did not produce sufficient national commitments to limit global warming to 1.5° Celsius by the end of the century, activists – including a significant proportion of young people – urged the parties to commit to more urgent, ambitious, and effective action. Such a response is a way out of the cul-de-sac of existing social orders which are problematic to the future and need to be challenged and turned around.

This more transformative worldview also indicates how people are not only reacting to the world but actively creating it through their actions. Such actions are co-constituting human development and the world itself. This approach emphasises the agency of individuals – including students – in shaping their lives and the world around them, and envisions a future where people can collectively create enhanced environments (Kemmis & Mahon, 2023).

At the same time as fostering a productive sense of agency, there is also a strong need to foster educational experiences that help to build a collective ethics of wellbeing. This includes ensuring not simply individual wellbeing, but the wellbeing of broader society and the physical environment upon which we are dependent for our survival. Kemmis and Mahon (2023) refer to the concept of critical praxis in education and research, emphasising the importance of creating 'worlds worth living in.' They argue that education should not only prepare individuals for future participation in society but also focus on bringing about the good for each person and humankind in general. Kemmis and Mahon (2023) further emphasise the need for deep listening, reflexive action, and responsiveness to context and culture in the pursuit of critical praxis. This is conceptualised as a 'transformative worldview,' where reality is constantly transformed and realised by people as active agents of social practices. Human endeavours are therefore seen as collaborative and co-constituted by individuals' active contributions to these practices, resulting in changes in both themselves and the world.

Miseliunaite et al. (2022) echo the need for education to encompass ethical interactions and wellbeing of the extended community. This is important within a broader context in which climate change is an ongoing and significant, indeed existential, issue. Drawing on Blyth and Meiring's (2018) notions of interactive ethical practices, Miseliunaite et al. (2022) highlighted the following key points:

- All actions have consequences.
- There is a need for respect for different points of view and constant dialogue with different members of the community.
- Environmental education requires 'being in the world.'
- Eco-education requires the simultaneous development of aesthetic and moral skills.
- Environmental education should be universal; it should be interdisciplinary and integrated into all subjects, and should be the basis for all education.

Indeed, education is a reciprocal process, in which students, teachers and the broader community impact their environment (cf. Bronfenbrenner, 1979), just as their environment impacts upon them; this is an active and recursive situation. Responding ethically entails understanding that learning environments need to include all members of the community and that many elements can enhance learning outcomes. We accord with Bloch's (1986) call for 'concrete utopias,' involving development of enhanced futures and more productive lives by analysing historical and social conditions/realities more overtly.

Key message: Educational sustainability integrates environmental sustainability and climate change topics into education, emphasising the active role of young people as agents in shaping their future.

Ways forward: It is important to advocate for a transformative view of education that fosters a collective ethics of wellbeing, promoting active participation in social movements for sustainable change.

2.8 Fostering equity

In relation to issues of equity and wellbeing, there are several approaches that should be taken into account to evaluate and monitor educational performance and provide targeted and/or intensive support where needed. The literature reveals several factors to help promote *equity* in schools. These include ensuring a culture characterised by the following:

- A belief that anyone can learn is a given.
- Every child has a right to early childhood education.
- Fair funding and resourcing must be provided to ensure all students have the opportunity to learn.
- Student and teacher wellbeing are paramount.

- Issues of health education and care (such as basic health, dental health, mental health, and counselling) must be considered.
- The curriculum must be balanced, involving a mix of disciplinary subjects as well as interdisciplinary topics, music, arts, physical activity, and play.
- There must be a broad-based approach that normalises and recognises all students as having learning needs.
- There must be articulation to broader government policies of social inclusion and youth and ability for young people to be included in decision-making over issues that concern them (Sahlberg, 2021; see *Appendix E* for further elaboration of each of these points).
- Greater attention must be given to Indigenous students and those lacking socio-economic resources.
- Career planning must be emphasised.
- Assessment of student achievement must be holistic (O'Connell et al., 2019).

In relation to AI and new technologies, there is also a need to remain vigilant to how engagement with new technologies is asymmetrical, with those from the most disadvantaged communities least able to access and maximise the use of such technologies. As Giannini (2023) argues, 'New technology implementation should prioritize the closing of equity gaps, not as an afterthought but a starting point' (p. 7).

Finally, even as various kinds of AI and other technologies may be proffered as 'solutions' to concerns about teacher shortages in hard-to-staff areas or disciplines, leading educational organisations will be those which sustain strong support for ongoing teacher learning and development to help address such shortages. Strong, equity-oriented systems will offer incentives for teachers to work in isolated and difficult-to-staff regions and communities, as well as drawing on the affordances of new technologies to help address geographic (and socio-economic) barriers to facilitate students' learning into the future.

Key message: Closing the equity gap is critical for maximising educational performance.

Ways forward: Adopting a multifaceted approach is important, including attention to beliefs about universal learning, education rights, fair funding, student and teacher wellbeing, social inclusion, and considerations for Indigenous and other minority students.

2.9 Chapter questions

1. Which part/s of the broader learning ecology in which you are working (system, school leadership, teaching, understanding of student learning/data) are operating most effectively to support student learning? Which aspects of this ecology require further development?

2. Within your organisation, which of the following areas require increased attention: school/system goal development, building teachers' capacity/capabilities, identification of student learning needs, and/or cultivating a culture that foregrounds student learning as its primary aim?

3. How 'balanced' is your school's/system's approach to enhancing student learning outcomes? Are you too focused on academic outcomes for their own sake, or do you use such outcomes to inform your understanding of what students have actually learned and a more holistic sense of student learning and development more broadly?

4. Outline some achievable objectives for maximising teachers' learning in your school or education system using Darling-Hammond et al.'s (2017) five key learning areas.

5. Reflect on the challenges of navigating new and existing educational technologies in your school or education system. What are the pros and cons associated with policies for implementing or limiting technologies such as generative AI, mobile/smart phones, personal devices, etc.?

6. How can your school/system embed wellbeing into your curriculum, policies, learning, and teaching sequences for a more holistic educational experience?

7. How could your curriculum design, school, learning community, or the education system more broadly empower student agency in promoting sustainable action in the community? What initiatives can teachers implement to inspire students to explore key global and local issues and contribute to society?

8. What specific initiatives could you and/or your school/system adopt to address issues related to a lack of equity in your community (or more broadly)? Can you identify key aspects of your school/system culture that could be modified to accommodate the needs of different groups of students, families and staff? Who feels included? Who is excluded?

2.10   References

Adolfsson, C.-H., & Håkansson, J. (2021). Data analysis for school improvement within coupled local school systems: Which data and with what purposes? *Leadership and Policy in Schools*, 1–14. https://doi.org/10.1080/15700763.2021.2010101

Alam, A. (2022). Investigating sustainable education and positive psychology interventions in schools towards achievement of sustainable happiness and wellbeing for 21st century pedagogy and curriculum. *ECS Transactions*, *107*(1), 19481–19494.

Balica, M. (2020). *Why wellbeing matters during a time of crisis wellbeing: Considerations for a successful post-Covid-19 educational transition*. International Baccalaureate Organization.

Bernhardt, V. L. (2016). *Data, data everywhere: Bringing all the data together for continuous school improvement*. Routledge.

Biddle, N., Edwards, B., Gray, M., & Sollis, K. (2021). *The impact of COVID-19 on child mental health and service barriers: The perspective of parents*. ANU Centre for Social Research and Methods, Australian National University.

Biesta, G. (2011). *Learning democracy in school and society: Education, lifelong learning and the politics of citizenship*. Brill.

Biesta, G. (2021). *World-centred education: A view for the present*. Routledge.

Bloch, E. (1986). *The principle of hope*. Basil Blackwell.

Blyth, C., & Meiring, R. (2018). A posthumanist approach to environmental education in South Africa: Implications for teachers, teacher development, and teacher training programs. *Teacher Development, 22*, 105–122.

Borland, J., & Charlton, A. (2020). The Australian labour market and the early impact of COVID-19: An assessment. *Australian Economic Review, 53*(3), 297–324.

Boylan, M., & Demack, S. (2018). Innovation, evaluation design and typologies of professional learning. *Educational Research, 60*(3), 336–356.

Brass, J., & Holloway, J. (2021). Re-professionalizing teaching: The new professionalism in the United States. *Critical Studies in Education, 62*(4), 519–536.

Brewer, J. (2014). Don't ban smartphones in Australian high schools: Here's why (and what we can do instead). *EduResearch Matters, Australian Association for Research in Education.* https://www.aare.edu.au/blog/?p=3066

Bronfenbrenner, U. (1979). *The ecology of human development: Experiments by nature and design.* Harvard University Press.

Brown, C., & Greany, T. (2018). The evidence-informed school system in England: Where should school leaders be focusing their efforts? *Leadership and Policy in Schools, 17*(1), 115–137.

Caine, G., & Caine, R. N. (2010). *Strengthening and enriching your professional learning community the art of learning together.* ASCD.

Campbell, M., & Edwards E. J. (2024, March 12). We looked at all the recent evidence on mobile phone bans in schools – this is what we found. *The Conversation.*https://theconversation.com/we-looked-at-all-the-recent-evidence-on-mobile-phone-bans-in-schools-this-is-what-we-found-224848

Cowan, C. D., Hauser, R. M., Levin, H. M., Beale Spencer, M., & Chapman, C. (2012). *Improving the measurement of socioeconomic status for the national assessment of educational progress: A theoretical foundation.* https://nces.ed.gov/nationsreportcard/pdf/researchcenter/Socioeconomic_Factors.pdf

Darling-Hammond, L., Burns, D., Campbell, C, Goodwin, A. L., Hammerness, K., Low, E-L., McIntyre, A., Sato, M., & Zeichner, K. (2017). *Empowered educators: How high-performing systems shape teaching quality around the world.* John Wiley & Sons.

Dimmock, C. (2019). Leading research-informed practice in schools. In D. Godfrey & C. Brown (Eds.), *An ecosystem for research-engaged schools* (pp. 56–72). Routledge.

Edwards, E. J., Taylor, C. S., & Vaughan, R. S. (2022). Individual differences in self-esteem and social anxiety predict problem smartphone use in adolescents. *School Psychology International, 43*(5), 460–476.

Ferreira, E., Silva, M. J., & Valente, D. C. (2018). *Collaborative uses of ICT in education: Practices and representations of preservice elementary school teachers.* International Symposium on Computers in Education (SIIE), Jerez, pp. 1–6.

Fullan, M. (2016). *The new meaning of educational change* (5th ed.). Teachers College Press.

Fullan, M., & Quinn, J. (2016). Coherence: The right drivers in action for schools, districts, and systems. *Teacher, 54*(5), 6.

Giannini, S. (2023). *Generative AI and the future of education.* UNESCO.

Goldsmith, B. (2014, October 27). *Media arts should be at the core of the Australian curriculum.* The Conversation. https://theconversation.com/media-arts-should-be-at-the-core-of-the-australian-curriculum-33401

Gore, J., Fray, L., Miller, A., Harris, J., & Taggart, W. (2021). The impact of COVID-19 on student learning in New South Wales primary schools: An empirical study. *The Australian Educational Researcher, 48*(4), 605–637.

Grassini, S. (2023). Shaping the future of education: Exploring the potential and consequences of AI and ChatGPT in educational settings. *Education Sciences, 13*(7), https://doi.org/10.3390/educsci13070692

Gravel, J., D'Amours-Gravel, M., & Osmanlliu, E. (2023). Learning to fake it: Limited responses and fabricated references provided by ChatGPT for medical questions. *Mayo Clinic Proceedings: Digital Health, 1*, 226–234.

Hardy, I., Hamid, M. O., & Reyes, V. (2020). The pragmatic perfectionism of educational policy: Reflections from Singapore. *Globalisation, Societies and Education, 19*(3), 355–370.

Hargreaves, A., & O'Connor, M. T. (2018). *Collaborative professionalism: When teaching together means learning for all*. Corwin Press.

Harris, A., & Jones, M. (2018). Leading schools as learning organizations. *School Leadership and Management, 38*(4), 351–354.

Hartong, S., & Förschler, A. (2019). Opening the black box of data-based school monitoring: Data infrastructures, flows and practices in state education agencies. *Big Data & Society, 6*(1). https://doi.org/10.1177/2053951719853533

Hitt, D. H., & Meyers, C. V. (2021). Examining three school systems' actions linked to improving their lowest-performing schools. *Leadership and Policy in Schools*. https://doi.org/10.1080/15700763.2021.1894454

Hollweck, T., & Lofthouse, R. M. (2021). Contextual coaching: Levering and leading school improvement through collaborative professionalism. *International Journal of Mentoring and Coaching in Education*. https://doi.org/10.1108/IJMCE-01-2021-0019

Kates, A. W., Wu, H., & Coryn, C. L. (2018). The effects of mobile phone use on academic performance: A meta-analysis. *Computers & Education, 127*, 107–112. https://doi.org/10.1016/j.compedu.2018.08.012

Kemmis, S., & Mahon, K. (2023). Finding worlds worth living in. In K. E. Reimer, M. Kaukko, S. Windsor, K. Mahon, & S. Kemmis (Eds.), *Living well in a world worth living in for all* (pp. 225–233). Springer. https://doi.org/10.1007/978-981-19-7985-9_12

Kessel, D., Lif Hardardottir, H., & Tyrefors, B. (2020). The impact of banning mobile phones in Swedish secondary schools. *Economics of Education Review, 77*, 1–11.

Kiilakoski, T., & Piispa, M. (2023). Facing the climate crisis, acting together: Young climate activists on building a sustainable future. In K. E. Reimer, M. Kaukko, S. Windsor, K. Mahon, & S. Kemmis (Eds.), *Living well in a world worth living in for all* (pp. 211–224). Springer. https://doi.org/10.1007/978-981-19-7985-9_12

Koh, K., & Luke, A. (2009). Authentic and conventional assessment in Singapore schools: An empirical study of teacher assignments and student work. *Assessment in Education: Principles, Policy & Practice, 16*(3), 291–318.

Kuss, D. J., Kanjo, E., Crook-Rumsey, M., Kibowski, F., Wang, G. Y., & Sumich, A. (2018). Problematic mobile phone use and addiction across generations: The roles of psychopathological symptoms and smartphone use. *Journal of Technology in Behavioural Science, 3*(3), 141–149.

Lee, D. H. L., Hong, H., & Niemi, H. (2014). A contextualized account of holistic education in Finland and Singapore: Implications on Singapore educational context. *The Asia-Pacific Education Researcher, 23*(4), 871–884.

Lingard, B. (2021). Enactments and resistances to globalizing testing regimes and performance-based accountability in the USA. In S. Grek, C. Maroy, & A. Verger (Eds.), *World yearbook of education 2021: Accountability and datafication in the governance of education* (pp. 257–271). Routledge.

Mayer, D., Dixon, M., Kline, J., Kostogriz, A., Moss, J., Rowan, L., Walker-Gibbs, B., & White, S. (2017). *Studying the effectiveness of teacher education: Early career teachers in diverse settings*. Springer.

McAleavy, T. et al. (2018). *Sustaining success: High performing government schools in London*. Education Development Trust.

Miseliunaite, B., Kliziene, I., & Cibulskas, G. (2022). Can holistic education solve the world's problems: A systematic literature review. *Sustainability (Basel, Switzerland), 14*(15), 9737.

Neumann, C. (2016). Teaching digital natives: Promoting information literacy and addressing instructional challenges. *Reading Improvement, 53*(3), 101–106.

Ng, P. T. (2017). *Learning from Singapore: The power of paradoxes*. Routledge.

Noble, K., Rehill, P., Sollis, K., Dakin, P., & Harris, D. (2021). *The wellbeing of Australian children: A story about data, a story about change*. UNICEF Australia & ARACY. www.

unicef.org.au/Upload/UNICEF/Media/Our%20work/Australia/The%20wellbeing%20 of%20Australia's%20children/Australian-Childrens-Wellbeing-Index-Report.pdf

O'Connell, M., Milligan, S. K., & Bentley, T. (2019). *Beyond ATAR: A proposal for change.* Koshland Innovation Fund.

Orlando, J. (2019, September 4). School phone ban is moral panic based on no evidence. *The Sydney Morning Herald.* https://www.smh.com.au/education/school-phone-ban-is-moral-panic-based-on-no-evidence-20190903-p52nnt.html

Pellegrino, J., Chudowsky, N., & Glaser, R. (2001). *Knowing what students know: The science and design of educational assessment.* National Academies Press.

Reyes, V., & Gopinathan, S. (2015). A critique of knowledge-based economies: A case study of Singapore stakeholders. *International Journal of Educational Reform, 24*(2), 136–159.

Reyes, V., & Tan, C. (2018). Assessment reforms in high-performing education systems: Shanghai and Singapore. In M. Khine (Ed.), *International trends in educational assessment: Emerging issues and practices* (pp. 25–37). Brill.

Sahlberg, P. (2020). We have a learning crisis but it's not about the kids. *Pasi Sahlberg Blog.* https://pasisahlberg.com/we-have-a-learning-crisis-but-its-not-about-the-kids/

Sahlberg, P. (2021). *Finnish lessons 3.0: What can the world learn from educational change in Finland?* (3rd ed.). Teachers College Press, Columbia University.

Schildkamp, K., Poortman, C., Luyten, H., & Ebbeler, J. (2017). Factors promoting and hindering data-based decision making in schools. *School Effectiveness and School Improvement, 28*(2), 242–258.

Selwyn, N., & Aagaard, J. (2021). Banning mobile phones from classrooms-an opportunity to advance understandings of technology addiction, distraction and cyberbullying. *British Journal of Educational Technology, 52*(1), 8–19.

Shen, X. (2007). *Shanghai education.* Thomson Learning.

Shepard, L. (2000). The role of assessment in a learning culture. *Educational Research, 29*(7), 4–14.

Sigurðardóttir, A. K., Hansen, B., & Gísladóttir, B. (2021). Development of an intervention framework for school improvement that is adaptive to cultural context. *Improving Schools,* 1–6. https://doi.org/10.1177/13654802211051929

Simmons, E. C., & Sanders, M. (2022). Building sustainable communities for sustainable development: An evidence-based behavior change intervention to reduce plastic waste and destructive fishing in Southeast Asia. *Sustainable Development, 30*(5), 1018–1029. https://doi.org/10.1002/sd.2296

Steiner-Khamsi, G. (2022). What is in a reference? Theoretically understanding the uses of evidence in education policy. In B. Karseth, K. Sivesend, & G. Steiner-Khamsi (Eds.), *Evidence and expertise in Nordic education policy: A comparative network analysis* (pp. 33–57). Palgrave Macmillan.

Stoll, L. (2020). Creating capacity for learning: Are we there yet? *Journal of Educational Change, 21,* 421–430.

Tan, C. (2013). *Learning from Shanghai: Lessons on achieving educational success.* Springer.

Tan, C. (2018). *Comparing high-performing education systems: Understanding Singapore, Shanghai, and Hong Kong.* Routledge.

Tan, C., & Reyes, V. (2018). Shanghai-China and the emergence of a global reference society. In L. Volante (Ed.), *The PISA effect on global educational governance* (pp. 61–75). Routledge.

Tan, K. (2022). Assessment reforms in Singapore. In Y.-J. Lee (Ed.), *Education in Singapore: People-making and nation-building* (pp. 243–260). Springer.

Tang, S. Y. F., & Cheng, M. M. H. (2021). Preparing high quality teacher education graduates in an era of unprecedented uncertainties: The case of Hong Kong. In D. Mayer (Ed.), *Teacher education policy and research: Global perspectives* (pp. 85–100). Springer.

UNESCO. (2020). *Education: From disruption to recovery.* https://en.unesco.org/covid19/educationresponse

Williamson, B. (2017). *Big data in education: The digital future of learning, policy and practice*. Sage.

Wong, A. K., Tang, S. Y., Li, D. D., & Cheng, M. M. (2021a). An exploratory study of teacher buoyancy. *Journal of Professional Capital & Community*, *6*(3), 281–297.

Wong, H. et al. (2021b). Changing assessments and the examination culture in singapore: A review and analysis of Singapore's assessment policies. *Asia Pacific Journal of Education*, *40*(4), 433–457.

3 Teacher expertise

Building teacher capability for impactful student learning

3.0 Introduction

Teaching excellence should be a priority for every education system, given 30% of the variance in student outcomes can be attributed to the work of teachers (Hattie, 2003). Further, the collective beliefs of teachers about their abilities to positively affect student outcomes in their school is one of the highest influences on student achievement (Visible Learning, 2017). Given perennial concerns about the high attrition rates of teachers, blamed on workload, teacher self-efficacy, and student behaviour, the chapter seeks to provide insights into the following:

1. The teaching and classroom management practices that have been shown to be the most impactful for lifting student learning outcomes;
2. The teaching and classroom management practices associated with improvements in student learning outcomes in particular demographic cohorts, including Indigenous (e.g., Aboriginal and Torres Strait Islander) students;
3. The most impactful ways of developing capability and building professional knowledge;
4. The systemic levers most effective in building teaching expertise once teachers have commenced their teaching careers and how these intersect with broader school improvement models, practices, and/or processes; and
5. Emerging competencies in which teachers require professional learning.

3.1 Impactful pedagogical and classroom management practices

Over recent years, there have been emergent research methodologies designed to measure 'what works' in education. Potentially the most widely cited of these studies has been the foundational work of Hattie (2009) and his ranking of educational practices based on their effect on student achievement. Mitchell (2020) extended the 'what works' concept to approaches used in special and inclusive education. In the US, the Department of Education funds the 'What Works Clearinghouse' as a repository for classroom teachers to locate evidence-based briefs and practice guides to help teachers in subject-specific domains (such as mathematics and science), general areas of capability (such as literacy and numeracy), teaching specific

DOI: 10.4324/9781032666839-3

learners (such as those with disability, who have English as an additional language, or who have behaviours requiring support), and students at different stages in their education. In December 2019, governments across Australia agreed to create an institute to provide Australian educators with access to evidence-based education research that demonstrates improved learning outcomes for all students. The Australian Education Research Organisation (AERO) was incorporated in 2021, and promotes research-informed approaches focused on classroom management, transitions, explicit instruction, family engagement for learning, formative assessment, mastery learning, spacing and retrieval, wellbeing for learning, and writing. Drawing from such sites is a useful starting point for teachers who typically may not have access to research that is published in journals that are 'hidden' behind publisher paywalls. This chapter begins by exploring teaching practices that support enhanced student learning outcomes.

3.1.1   *Pedagogical practices that work*

The Centre for Education Statistics and Evaluation (2020) identified eight evidence-based teaching strategies as important for impacting student outcomes. These include high expectations, explicit teaching, effective feedback, use of data to inform practice, assessment, classroom management, wellbeing, and collaboration. In addition, the report mentioned the Victorian Department of Education and Training's *High Impact Teaching Strategies* (2020). This *HITS* model, which has been adopted and refined by a range of jurisdictions across Australia, also highlights the importance of explicit teaching, feedback, and collaborative learning, as well as referring to goal setting, structured lessons, providing worked examples, questioning, offering students multiple exposure, teaching metacognitive strategies, and differentiated teaching as important foci.

For students with diverse learning needs, practices such as providing adjustments, differentiation, responsive teaching, using data to identify disparities in academic achievement, building effective relationships, and addressing deficits in curriculum design and pedagogical approaches are all noted as effective. There is also an increasing need for teachers to engage with digital pedagogies (fast-tracked significantly in some settings during the COVID-19 pandemic), through the promotion of the TPACK model for integrating technology into classroom practices.

Gomendio (2017) asserts that educational systems around the world that have succeeded in lifting student performance share one common trait: they have made teachers their top priority. She recommended high-quality education systems need to focus on both sustainable excellence and equity. Teachers need support to ensure high standards from all students, particularly regarding the increasing diversity in their classrooms. Gomendio (2017) suggests education systems should proactively address factors known to impede student performance, such as historical practices that have reinforced barriers, perpetuated stereotypes, and fostered inaccurate perceptions related to students' socio-economic backgrounds, gender, identity, abilities/disability, and ethnicity/language backgrounds.

3.1.2   *Classroom management practices*

The use of evidence-based, high leverage classroom management practices has been demonstrated to increase engagement, achievement, and positive behaviour amongst students (Korpershoek et al., 2016). Despite this, traditional pre-service and in-service training have proven insufficient in supporting teachers to transfer this research into sustained classroom practice (Goss et al., 2015; O'Neill & Stephenson, 2014). The ability of teachers to deliver high-impact teaching is limited if they are unskilled in eliciting engagement from students. Considerable research cites the work of Fredricks (2013), proposing that teachers can support student engagement by showing students that they care, providing a positive social environment, having clear expectations, and creating activities that have real-world application so that students can make sense of their learning. Teachers need to be able to effectively respond to student behaviour to have high-impact teaching, but, further, teachers need to be able to effectively engage all learners to prevent problematic behaviours in the first instance (Poed et al., 2020).

Bowsher et al. (2018) found that 80% of recent graduates feel confident in teaching their subject content compared to only 55% who feel well-prepared to manage their classroom and address disciplinary issues. To build confidence, Hirsch et al. (2021) recommended teachers must be skilled in designing the physical layout of classrooms; setting clear expectations for behaviours; establishing clear rules and routines; maximising instructional time, using approaches such as opportunities to respond and active supervision; having positive teacher-student interactions; positively acknowledging students, using contingent behaviour-specific praise and reinforcement; and responding to behaviours of concern through tactical ignoring, functional understanding of behaviour, and differential reinforcement. Hirsch et al. (2021) proposed a practice-based professional development framework recommending that teachers engage with others who have similar needs, that professional learning be contextualised to what the teacher needs, and that any professional learning provide opportunities for modelling, independent practice, and feedback.

Paramita et al. (2020) explored the professional learning needs of teachers, beyond graduates, and recognised that behaviour support constitutes a significant component of a teacher's workday. Paramita et al. (2020) examined both the characteristics of effective professional learning that can improve classroom management as well as the impact this has on teachers' knowledge and practice. The authors concluded that there is an important place for in-service professional learning for classroom teachers to bridge the research-to-practice gap. Further, if a system wants to raise the skills of teachers on a specific classroom management approach (such as how to give behaviour-specific praise), then brief didactic training can be effective, but if the focus is on helping teachers and school leaders develop a more comprehensive behaviour support system, a more comprehensive array of professional learning implementation strategies is needed to bring about teacher change.

> **Key message**: Prioritising the needs of classroom teachers is the key to improving student learning outcomes. Teachers need synthesised access to information on evidence-based, high-impact classroom management and teaching practices if they are to lift student performance.
>
> **Ways forward**: A comprehensive array of professional learning opportunities is more effective than brief didactic professional learning.

3.2 Tailoring instructional and support practices for diverse demographic cohorts

The United Nations (2015) Sustainable Development Goals (SDGs), as part of the 2030 Agenda for Sustainable Development, set a global education agenda to ensure inclusive and quality education for all and to promote lifelong learning. This ambitious goal has a direct impact on the already multifaceted role of teachers; consequently, there are many competing factors in facilitating a classroom to cater for different student cohorts. There may be strategies and pedagogies that teachers will use to engage and improve outcomes for students. However, communities are diverse and what works in some communities may not work in others; having relationships with and knowing students and community are important to improving outcomes using a strengths-based approach (Phillips, 2021).

3.2.1 *Tailoring for students with disability and diverse learning needs*

Classrooms around the world comprise students who bring different home backgrounds, different abilities, and different identities. Historically, schools responded to student diversity through separate provisions for anyone who was viewed as different, including separate 'special' schools, separate classrooms which shared the same school grounds, separate curriculum, and so on (de Bruin, 2018). For many diverse learners, this led to them being given a diluted educational experience (Cruz, 2021). Over time, schools have been seen as a lynchpin in creating inclusive societies (Richardson, 1998; Thomas, 2020), and in today's educational landscape, the diverse array of students in inclusive classrooms is increasingly evident and celebrated. A critical ingredient in the success of these classrooms sustaining inclusion is the capacity of teachers to tailor their pedagogical and classroom management approaches to meet the needs of all learners. Through recognition of the uniqueness and strengths of each student as well as the provision of adjustments to the environment, the content being taught, the teaching strategies, the assessment approaches, and the ways in which students are able to engage with one another, all students have an equal opportunity to participate and demonstrate their learning on the same basis.

An initial critical step for teachers is to be able to recognise the diversity within their classrooms, including the varying backgrounds, differing abilities and strengths, and how each of these might shape their learning. Teachers need to be culturally responsive and relevant in their teaching, recognising and understanding the differing cultural norms, perspectives, and values of students, and how these can enrich learning (Chang & Viesca, 2022). They need to ensure equity and access for all students, ensuring that where students live or what resources they have access to outside of school does not limit the educational opportunities they can access through school. Teachers then need to look at how they can cultivate inclusive classrooms, teaching empathy, respect, and other values important to an inclusive society.

To support schools in this important work, some staff have adopted the Multi-Tiered Systems of Support (MTSS) approach based on its effectiveness and efficiency (Kern et al., 2020). MTSS is a framework that facilitates school staff identifying three tiers of support needed to facilitate the inclusion of all learners. At the first tier, staff identify academic, behavioural, and social-emotional practices that have been demonstrated, through research, to be effective in supporting the inclusion of most students. These universal practices typically meet the needs of around 80–85% of the school population. Tier 1 of an MTSS framework is critical. Historically, teachers would use one set of approaches, sometimes not grounded in research, to teach their class, and any student for whom these approaches were ineffective were then referred for testing, additional support, or potentially referral to another setting (Gresham, 2007). Within Tier 1 of MTSS, teachers are not waiting for students to fail and then referring them out of the classroom but are instead embedding consistent, evidence-based practices designed to support the inclusion of all learners (Fuchs et al., 2003; Scruggs & Mastropieri, 2002).

Once these practices are in place, and being implemented with fidelity, staff then identify a second tier of supports to supplement Tier 1 that are targeted at learners for whom the first tier of practices were insufficient in supporting their full inclusion (Poed & de Bruin, 2022). Again, these practices are supported by research as effective in meeting the needs of a further 10–15% of students. Finally, after embedding Tiers 1 and 2, there may still be some students who need highly individualised or intensive support to meet their academic, social-emotional, or behavioural needs. At Tier 3, these students are provided with support at greater frequency or intensity to meet their individualised needs (Adamson et al., 2019).

MTSS evolved from other well-known educational approaches, such as response to intervention (RTI) and Positive Behavioural Interventions and Supports (PBIS) (Mahoney, 2020). RTI used the same three-tiered approach, initially to identify students at risk of reading difficulty, but expanded later to include other areas of literacy and numeracy and then academic skills more broadly. Later, the RTI model was extended to consider how the behavioural and social-emotional needs of learners could be supported in tandem, and the PBIS framework emerged to specifically target these skills. The two models (RTI and PBIS) are grounded in the same science: prevention science and implementation science (Lane et al., 2020). These two fields of inquiry seek to understand how best to prevent education systems from failing children, and how to implement changes that allow all children to thrive. When merged, RTI and PBIS form one framework known as MTSS. MTSS provides the framework that allows schools to create a climate of inclusion.

Once a climate of inclusion has been created, the next step is to consider how the content and teaching can be inclusive. Universal Design for Learning (UDL) is a framework used by educators as part of MTSS or can be used as a standalone framework. UDL has gained prominence as a guide for designing content and planning lessons that minimise barriers for diverse learners (Baglieri, 2020). Teachers who adopt the framework are urged to consider the multiple ways in which they can teach the content of a lesson, engage students in the learning, and assess what students have learnt. The design principles that underpin the framework shift the gaze of teachers from a deficit lens, where students who learn differently to their peers are viewed as the problem, to focusing more explicitly on how the curriculum or pedagogy might serve as barriers to learning for some students.

3.2.2   *Tailoring for Indigenous/Aboriginal and Torres Strait Islander students*

Indigenous education, including Aboriginal and Torres Strait Islander education, should also come from a strengths-based approach; however, education literature generally reinforces a poor outlook in relation to outcomes for Indigenous peoples, including Aboriginal and Torres Strait Islander peoples (Shay & Miller, 2021). Changes in the way Aboriginal and Torres Strait Islander education, perspectives, and knowledges are viewed by staff members play an important role in fostering improvements (Shay & Miller, 2021) and need to be developed from a whole-school approach, via the school leadership team and involving community input (Barber et al., 2019). Current research shows that schooling for marginalised students persistently causes ongoing systemic harm, including experiences of alienation, negative self-concept, and trauma (Moodie, 2019). Strengths-based approaches have been around for some time in countries such as Australia but are often not promoted in an Aboriginal and Torres Strait Islander context due to the political, social, and racial constructs of Australia that are often played out in the media and policy (Shay & Oliver, 2021). A strengths-based approach can be a highly effective method for shifting or changing narratives in Aboriginal and Torres Strait Islander education, and Indigenous education more broadly.

One way to address this shift to a strengths-based approach that aligns with the literature is to invite Aboriginal and Torres Strait Islander community members into the school to work in partnership with educators. Research tells us about the importance of working with community and how valuable the input of community members is to embed and implement Aboriginal and Torres Strait Islander perspectives and knowledges in schools to support student learning outcomes. Working together, educators and Aboriginal and Torres Strait Islander community members can co-construct curriculum and learning experiences to combine knowledge and practice with specific community understanding (Armour & Miller, 2021). Such co-construction enriches the learning for everyone (all teachers, students) as well as meeting the cultural and educational needs of Aboriginal and Torres Strait Islander students (Schulz et al., 2023). Of course, these contributions by Aboriginal and Torres Strait Islander peoples should be completed in a paid capacity. Additionally, it is important that strong and reciprocal relationships are developed. Having local Aboriginal and Torres Strait Islander communities input their knowledges and perspectives supports schools by providing a culturally safe space (Andersen et al., 2015). Students can feel culturally safe knowing that local knowledges and perspectives have been provided by community members and learning experiences have been co-constructed so that there is minimal room for misappropriation. The outcomes of this co-construction of the curriculum can be shared in an informal setting, such as a relaxed meeting, or in a more formal setting, such as a professional learning activity.

Educators' knowledge, learning, and skills can be improved with professional learning, which can also support them to shift their ways of thinking so that they encourage all students to thrive. Focusing on strengths-based approaches, Buxton's (2020) study consisted of primary school teachers participating in two days of professional learning, with Aboriginal educators leading the first day and focusing on the concept and meaning of Country from their worldview. They guided participants through the content learning experiences using Aboriginal perspectives and knowledges. The second day consisted of follow-up in-school workshops to assist participant teachers to design learning and teaching approaches, tailoring those concepts into strategies and activities for the children in their classes at various levels and based on a mentor/peer learning approach. For the professional learning sessions, Buxton (2020) used a framework *Yurunnhang Bungil Nyumba* (learn respect to teach), which was written based on an understanding that people each learn what they can, according to their own growth and development. This framework allows the teacher to be guided and learn from Country. While more 'formal' modes of professional development are important, connecting to Country and building relationships with the community are also key elements in this framework so that teachers and students have a safe environment in which to learn (Buxton, 2020).

There have been many studies relating to Aboriginal and Torres Strait Islander education that have presented key research findings in the literature that continue to emerge time and time again. Luke et al. (2013) provide a useful account of such findings when they present the following:

- High value placed on education by Aboriginal and Torres Strait Islander peoples;
- Low recognition and acknowledgement by schools and teachers of the social and cultural values of Aboriginal and Torres Strait Islander children and youth;
- Low engagement of schools and teachers with local Indigenous peoples and communities;
- Strong support for the inclusion of Indigenous knowledges and perspectives into the curriculum from teachers who report regular social and community engagement with Indigenous peoples; however, teachers report a lack of knowledge and cultural experience to teach in this field;

- High levels of deficit perspectives of Aboriginal and Torres Strait Islander children, families, and communities informing classroom practice, including classroom management; and
- Less time spent on classroom management and in the teaching of basic skills in the classrooms of more experienced teachers (>10 years) (Luke et al., 2013).

Barber et al. (2019) reported on the Association of Independent Schools (AIS-NSW) pilot project to support schools to improve outcomes for Indigenous students. The project's goals were embedded in the Australian Government's *Students First* agenda and underpinned by the priorities of the *National Aboriginal and Torres Strait Islander Education Strategy* (Australian Government [Department of Education], 2015), with a focus on providing quality teaching and quality learning. The project found that participating schools succeeded in improving Indigenous students' literacy and numeracy outcomes, as well as other academic-related outcomes. How the schools achieved these outcomes varied according to their unique context and school community, yet there were common identifiable strategies across all projects. The nine strategies identified ranged from building relationships to including Aboriginal and Torres Strait Islander perspectives within the school using a whole-school approach to change culture with regards to improving Aboriginal and Torres Strait Islander student outcomes. Included in the project findings were key enablers and challenges and 16 recommendations. The recommendations provide a strong basis for future directions at both the individual school and wider sector levels, including for sustainability and scaling up of strategies and activities to improve Indigenous students' academic and other outcomes.

Burgess et al. (2019) conducted a systematic review of literature focusing on pedagogies that support, engage, and improve the educational outcomes of Aboriginal students. Similar to points outlined earlier, they found equity issues such as low teacher expectations of Aboriginal students, a focus on classroom management resulting in 'defensive' teaching and lower levels of culturally responsive approaches to curriculum and pedagogy that required further attention. Other studies, such as Donovan (2015) and Lewthwaite et al. (2015), pointed out similar deficiencies regarding evidence of effective pedagogies, but they also noted that Aboriginal voices and perspectives are often excluded from the research. This supports suggestions that low expectations and deficit thinking permeate policy and practice for disadvantaged students including Aboriginal and Torres Strait Islander learners.

To move forward from the key research findings and in alignment with professional teaching standards and nation-specific initiatives, such as the Australian *Alice Springs (Mparntwe) Education Declaration* (Education Council, 2019), all schools should adopt a holistic approach to include and embed Indigenous/Aboriginal and Torres Strait Islander perspectives and knowledges from a local, regional, and national standpoint. These perspectives and knowledges need to be embedded in schools regardless of whether Indigenous/Aboriginal and Torres Strait Islander students are enrolled. A holistic approach to implementing these perspectives and knowledges is needed, including adapting the curriculum to localised learning, knowing students, professional learning, community collaboration, mentoring and working alongside teachers as equal leaders to craft curriculum, and delivering key lessons that cultivate greater understanding (Bishop & Vass, 2021). Autonomy is also required and education systems including teachers and principals need to surrender their historic power to allow a level playing field for Indigenous/Aboriginal perspectives and knowledges to be embedded (Bishop & Vass, 2021).

Key message: Students are not vulnerable because of a condition, personal circumstances, or backgrounds. Vulnerability occurs because of inequity within the system and policies and practices that contribute to marginalisation.

Ways forward: Professional learning that aids teachers to adopt a strengths-based focus is essential to lift learning outcomes for all learners, including Indigenous/Aboriginal and Torres Strait Islander students. Adopting culturally responsive and relevant, evidence-informed practices and embedding Indigenous/Aboriginal and Torres Strait Islander perspectives and knowledges are critical for improving outcomes.

3.3   Developing capability and building professional knowledge

Around the world, government education jurisdictions have developed dedicated models or policies to support teacher professional knowledge, including the creation of dedicated centres to support the delivery of career-long, online, and face-to-face teacher professional learning. Professional learning for early career teachers provided by departments of education appears to be more oriented to classroom management, planning, and administrative duties (Kyndt et al., 2016). Literature relating to the professional learning requirements of mid-career teachers is sparse. Findings suggest that teachers who are mid-career typically want to develop expertise in specific areas, such as new instructional methods or leadership skills required for career progression rather than general classroom management; they seek teacher-driven rather than compulsory professional learning and assign greater importance to classroom-based action research than teachers in other career stages do (Booth et al., 2021; Cawte, 2020; Kyndt et al., 2016).

Knight and Cooper (2019) have proposed an alternative to simple professional learning sessions for teachers. Instead, they recommend within-school peer coaching as a feasible, acceptable, and contextually relevant approach to build teacher capabilities and professional knowledge. The authors challenged the $8B investment spent during 2015 by the 50 largest education districts in the United States. They found, despite the effort and money expended, there was little impact on classroom practice. Instead, they proposed that teacher expertise is increased through an instructional coaching model, where a teacher is partnered with an instructional coach to identify a learning goal and strategies to achieve the goal. The coach then provides modelling to assist the teacher achieve their goal, and the teacher is given opportunities to practice with guidance and feedback from the instructional coach until the goal is met. When teachers learn new strategies in the context of their work, they are likely to facilitate higher educational outcomes for students and greater wellbeing. Within-school peer coaching, through establishing mini in-school professional learning communities, is a feasible, acceptable, and contextually relevant approach to build teacher capabilities for effective classroom management and student inclusion (Joyce & Calhoun, 2019; Knight & Cooper, 2019).

Within an Australian context, Telfer (2020) also examined the benefits of a within-school peer coaching model on teachers' use of evidence-based classroom management and instructional strategies that are shown, through research, to enhance student engagement and behaviour. She posited that traditional in-service training is inadequate for facilitating teachers' sustained adoption of new knowledge and application of new skills in the classroom. Instead, she found that coaching teachers to set goals and then providing performance feedback from peer-coaching observations offered a promising approach for increasing teachers' use of evidence-based practices. Further, following surveys of teachers involved in her study, Telfer found that they regarded peer-coaching as both feasible and effective in changing their classroom practices.

Darling-Hammond et al. (2017) also acknowledge that professional development provided to classroom teachers is mostly ineffective in changing their practice in classrooms or on impacting student learning outcomes. However, they were able to identify 35 studies that demonstrated a positive link between attendance at professional development and changed teaching practice and student outcomes. Synthesising the shared features of these professional learning activities, the authors contend that professional development that is content-focused, incorporates active learning, supports teacher collaboration, incorporates modelling of effective practice, provides coaching and expert support, offers feedback and direction, and is sustained over time enable effective professional learning that builds teacher expertise and drives better outcomes for students.

Another common approach to building teacher capacity is through within-school and cross-school professional learning communities. Vangrieken et al. (2017) contend that, for the past three decades, schools have been using different types of professional learning communities as a solution to providing professional learning for areas where traditional professional learning has failed to change practice. They acknowledge that there are five key characteristics of effective professional learning communities. These are supportive and shared leadership; shared vision, values, and goals; opportunities for collective learning and application; sharing of individual practice through discussion, modelling, and observations; and the physical and human resources to support implementation. They argue the most critical features for success are supportive leadership, the composition of and dynamics amongst the group, and trust and respect.

> **Key message**: Professional learning requirements for teachers may dif-
> fer significantly at various career stages. Stand-alone didactic professional
> learning has limited impact on addressing these needs or on changing teacher
> practice. Systematic reviews of literature have identified critical characteris-
> tics of successful professional learning approaches.
>
> **Ways forward**: Instructional coaching, modelling, independent practice
> (followed by feedback, peer coaching, and collaboration), and active learn-
> ing (supplemented by leadership support and adequate resourcing) are shown
> to improve teacher expertise and change classroom practice.

3.4   Systemic levers for building teaching expertise

Kirsten (2020) offers the view that no intervention designed to bring about school
improvement will produce sustainable gains in student achievement (even when
all the features of high-quality professional learning are in place) unless there is a
recognition that when a system needs to make deep and lasting change, learning is
essential. That is, professional development on its own is insufficient without the
support structures to ensure success; professional learning must target both teachers and school leaders since teachers rely on their leadership team to translate and
adapt education policy for the local school context (Kirsten, 2020). The earlier
cited paper by Darling-Hammond and colleagues (2017) notes seven additional
key systemic levers for effective professional learning for teachers. These include
the following:

1. The development of standards to guide the design and support the evaluation
   of both internally provided and externally sourced professional development
   activities;
2. Ensuring time is built into the school day to allow teachers opportunities for professional learning, peer coaching and observations, and collaborative planning;
3. Regular needs assessments to ensure that centrally delivered professional learning aligns with what teachers believe they need to demonstrate excellence in
   their classrooms;
4. Identifying and developing classroom teachers who can serve as mentors or
   coaches;
5. Ensuring adequate professional learning is aligned to new policies/initiatives,
   focused on the expertise needed by the teacher to deliver the initiative in their
   school;
6. Considering ways to ensure, particularly for those in rural and remote locations, that technology-facilitated opportunities for professional learning are
   offered; and
7. Establishing flexible funding models as well as continuing education units that
   allow for sustained collaboration opportunities, mentoring, coaching, and professional learning activities.

In light of the insights provided by Kirsten (2020) and the research by Darling-Hammond and colleagues (2017), it is clear that sustainable improvements in student achievement within a school system necessitate a multifaceted approach to teachers' learning. Professional development, while valuable, is insufficient on its own; it must be complemented by robust support structures. This support should extend to both teachers and school leaders since effective translation and adoption of education policies to local contexts depend upon leadership. Additionally, Darling-Hammond's seven systemic leavers underscore the importance of standards, dedicated time for professional learning and collaboration, needs assessments, mentorship, alignment with policies, technology-facilitated opportunities, and flexible funding models. Implementing these principles can lay a foundation for meaningful and lasting educational change.

Key message: For the system to make deep and lasting change to student outcomes, an investment in school leaders and teachers is essential. Effective instructional coaching and professional learning communities can enhance teachers' capacity to support students' learning needs.

Ways forward: A return on investment in professional learning for teachers is only possible where systemic levers for professional learning are given equal consideration to the content of, and models used to deliver, professional learning programs.

3.5 Emerging competencies in which teachers require professional learning

A wide range of varied topics related to emerging competencies where teachers may require professional learning have been identified in relevant literature. For example, Tabach and Trgalová (2019) suggested teachers need pedagogical technological knowledge to embed digital technologies in classrooms to create digitally literate learners. Sharma (2018) proposed that Australian teachers need better knowledge of how to work in inclusive classrooms, citing pre-service teacher education foci on the 'what' of inclusive education but with less attention to the 'how.' Jackson et al. (2021) argued that a specific requirement of teachers in supporting learners with disability is knowing how to lead the work of teacher aides. Jurkowski et al. (2020) suggested that teachers need to learn more about how to successfully implement co-teaching as a resource for supporting inclusive classes. Mahmud and Satchell (2022) suggested teachers need to learn more about how to promote mental wellbeing in young people.

The issue of out-of-field teaching attracted considerable attention in the literature. According to an Australian study conducted by Weldon (2016), 26% of junior secondary teachers and 15% of senior secondary teachers are required to teach subjects which they have not studied beyond first year at university and for which they have not studied teaching pedagogy. Further, Weldon found early career teachers are far more likely to be asked to teach out of field (37%) compared to teachers with five or more years of experience (25%). As an equity issue, Weldon identified that 26% of classes in remote locations compared to 14% in metropolitan locations, and 19% of classes taught in low socioeconomic schools versus 13% in higher socio-economic settings, were taught by an out-of-field teacher. It is unsurprising, therefore, that the literature recommends professional learning in content knowledge for these teachers. This is the case for teachers across the board who teach out-of-field, including those who teach in the areas of English (Caldis, 2017), science (Hobbs, 2020), mathematics (O'Meara & Faulkner, 2021), geography (Caldis & Kleeman, 2019), health and physical education (Barwood et al., 2017), and special education (Hobbs et al., 2020).

Key message: There are a range of areas in which teachers, particularly early career teachers and those in remote or low-socioeconomic areas, need further professional development. It is crucial that those teachers who are required to teach in areas they have not studied have access to further professional learning in both content and pedagogical skills. Without this, there will be ongoing equity and effectiveness issues in education.

Ways forward: To address this challenge, one proposed solution is to identify teachers who need professional learning and provide targeted and comprehensive professional learning for teachers in areas where they are teaching out-of-field using the array of professional learning approaches proposed in the previous section. This professional learning should focus on both content knowledge and pedagogical skills, ensuring that teachers are better prepared to deliver quality, equitable educational opportunities. Additionally, educational institutions (including universities) and policymakers need to work together to provide incentives and support for teachers in remote or low-socioeconomic areas to acquire the necessary knowledge and skills to teach effectively in these contexts, thereby promoting equitable access to quality education for all students, regardless of where they live.

3.6   Chapter questions

1. How have recent repositories like the What Works Clearinghouse or the Australian Educational Research Organisation influenced your, or your school's, adoption of evidence-based teaching strategies?
2. How can schools, or other educational institutions, bridge the gap between evidence-based, high-impact practices and their effective implementation by teachers?
3. What are the key elements of professional development and support that can empower you, or teachers in your school, to improve practices, engage students, and prevent barriers that impede student learning?

4. What specific changes or strategies could your school, or education system more broadly, use to effectively transition from a deficit-focused approach to a strengths-based approach in the education of diverse learners?
5. How could your school, or the education system more broadly, adapt their approach to teacher professional learning to better meet the diverse needs of early-career, mid-career, and highly experienced teachers? Are there limitations to the professional learning approaches currently being used?

3.7   References

Adamson, R. M., McKenna, J. W., & Mitchell, B. (2019). Supporting all students: Creating a tiered continuum of behavior support at the classroom level to enhance schoolwide multi-tiered systems of support. *Preventing School Failure: Alternative Education for Children and Youth, 63*(1), 62–67.

Andersen, C., Gower, L., & O'Dowd, M. (2015). *Aboriginal education workers in Tasmania becoming teachers, more Aboriginal and Torres Strait Islander teachers initiative (MAT-SITI).* http://ecite.utas.edu.au/110531/

Armour, D., & Miller, J. (2021). Relational pedagogies and co-constructing curriculum. In *Indigenous education in Australia* (pp. 162–173). Routledge.

Australian Government [Department of Education]. (2015). *National Aboriginal and Torres Strait Islander education strategy.* www.education.gov.au/indigenous-education/national-aboriginal-and-torres-strait-islander-education-strategy

Baglieri, S. (2020). Toward inclusive education? Focusing a critical lens on universal design for learning. *Canadian Journal of Disability Studies, 9*(5), 42–74.

Barber, T., Behrendt, L., & Graham, M. (2019). *AISNSW pilot project: Improving outcomes for Aboriginal and Torres Strait Islander students-final evaluation report.* Association of Independent Schools of New South Wales.

Barwood, D., Penney, D., & Cunningham, C. (2017). A paradox or a culture of acceptance? The idiosyncratic workforce delivering health education in lower secondary government schools in Western Australia. *Asia-Pacific Journal of Health, Sport and Physical Education, 8*(3), 193–209.

Bishop, M., & Vass, G. (2021). Talking about culturally responsive approaches to education: Teacher professional learning, indigenous learners and the politics of schooling. *The Australian Journal of Indigenous Education, 50*(2), 340–347.

Booth, J., Coldwell, M., Müller, L. M., Perry, E., & Zuccollo, J. (2021). Mid-career teachers: A mixed methods scoping study of professional development, career progression and retention. *Education Sciences, 11*(6), 299–332.

Bowsher, A., Sparks, D., & Mulvaney Hoyer, K. (2018, April). *Preparation and support for teachers in public schools: Reflections on the first year of teaching. Stats in brief.* U.S. Department of Education. https://files.eric.ed.gov/fulltext/ED581881.pdf

Burgess, C., Tennent, C., Vass, G., Guenther, J., Lowe, K., & Moodie, N. (2019). A systematic review of pedagogies that support, engage and improve the educational outcomes of Aboriginal students. *The Australian Educational Researcher, 46*, 297–318.

Buxton, L. M. (2020). Professional development for teachers meeting cross-cultural challenges. *Journal for Multicultural Education.* www.emerald.com/insight/content/doi/10.1108/JME-06-2019-0050/full/html

Caldis, S. (2017). Teaching out of field: Teachers having to know what they do not know. *Geography Bulletin, 49*(1), 13–17. https://researchers.mq.edu.au/en/publications/teaching-out-of-field-teachers-having-to-know-what-they-do-not-know

Caldis, S., & Kleeman, G. (2019). Out-of-field teaching in geography. *Geographical Education (Online), 32*, 11–14.

Cawte, K. (2020). Teacher crisis: Critical events in the mid-career stage. *Australian Journal of Teacher Education, 45*(8), 75–92.

Centre for Education Statistics and Evaluation. (2020). *What works best: 2020 update*. NSW Government – Department of Education. https://education.nsw.gov.au/about-us/educational-data/cese/publications/research-reports/what-works-best-2020-update

Chang, W. C., & Viesca, K. M. (2022). Preparing teachers for culturally responsive/relevant pedagogy (CRP): A critical review of research. *Teachers College Record, 124*(2), 197–224.

Cruz, K. E. (2021). *Strategies for stressed teachers to solve challenges in the diverse classroom* [Masters dissertation, Thompson Rivers University]. https://arcabc.ca/islandora/object/tru%3A5735/datastream/PDF/view

Darling-Hammond, L., Burns, D., Campbell, C, Goodwin, A. L., Hammerness, K., Low, E-L., McIntyre, A., Sato, M., & Zeichner, K. (2017). *Empowered educators: How high-performing systems shape teaching quality around the world*. John Wiley & Sons.

de Bruin, K. (2018). *Differentiation in the classroom: Engaging diverse learners through universal design for learning*. https://research.monash.edu/files/264002785/255280204_oa.pdf

Donovan, M. J. (2015). Aboriginal student stories, the missing voice to guide us towards change. *Australian Educational Researcher, 42*(5), 613–625.

Education Council. (2019). *Alice springs (Mparntwe) education declaration*. https://docs.education.gov.au/documents/alice-springs-mparntwe-educationdeclaration

Fredricks, J. (2013). Behavioral engagement in learning. In J. Hattie & E. Anderman (Eds.), *International guide to student achievement* (pp. 42–44). Routledge/Taylor & Francis Group.

Fuchs, D., Mock, D., Morgan, P. L., & Young, C. L. (2003). Responsiveness-to-intervention: Definitions, evidence, and implications for the learning disabilities construct. *Learning Disabilities Research & Practice, 18*, 157–171.

Gomendio, M. (2017). *Empowering and enabling teachers to improve equity and outcomes for all*. OECD Publishing. www.oecd-ilibrary.org/education/empowering-and-enabling-teachers-to-improve-equity-and-outcomes-for-all_9789264273238-en

Goss, P., Hunter, J., Romanes, D., & Parsonage, H. (2015). *Targeted teaching: How better use of data can improve student learning*. Grattan Institute. https://grattan.edu.au/report/targeted-teaching-how-better-use-of-data-can-improve-student-learning/

Gresham, F. M. (2007). Evolution of the response-to-Intervention concept: Empirical foundations and recent developments. In S. R. Jimerson, M. K. Burns, & A. M. vander Heyden (Eds.), *Handbook of response to intervention: The science and practice of assessment and intervention* (pp. 10–24). Springer.

Hattie, J. A. C. (2003). *Teachers make a difference: What is the research evidence?* Paper presented at the Building Teacher Quality: What does the Research Tell Us? ACER Research Conference, Melbourne, Australia. http://research.acer.edu.au/research_conference_2003/4/

Hattie, J. A. C. (2009). *Visible learning: A synthesis of over 800 meta-analyses relating to achievement*. Routledge.

Hirsch, S. E., Randall, K., Bradshaw, C., & Lloyd, J. W. (2021). Professional learning and development in classroom management for novice teachers: A systematic review. *Education and Treatment of Children, 44*(4), 291–307.

Hobbs, L. (2020). Learning to teach science out-of-field: A spatial-temporal experience. *Journal of Science Teacher Education, 31*, 725–745.

Hobbs, L., Hartley, C., Bentley, S., Bibby, J., Bowden, L., Hartley, J., & Stevens, C. (2020). Shared special interest play in a specific extra-curricular group setting: A Minecraft club for children with special educational needs. *Educational and Child Psychology, 37*(4), 81–95.

Jackson, C., Sharma, U., Odier-Guedj, D., & Deppeler, J. (2021). Teachers' perceptions of their work with teacher assistants: A systematic literature review. *Australian Journal of Teacher Education, 46*(11). https://ro.ecu.edu.au/ajte/vol46/iss11/5/

Joyce, B., & Calhoun, E. F. (2019). Peer coaching in education. In S. J. Zepeda & J. A. Ponticell (Eds.), *The Wiley handbook of educational supervision* (pp. 307–328).

Jurkowski, S., Ulrich, M., & Muller, B. (2020). Co-teaching as a resource for inclusive classes: Teachers' perspectives on conditions for successful collaboration. *International Journal of Inclusive Education.* Advance online publication. https://doi.org/10.1080/136 03116.2020.1821449

Kern, L., McIntosh, K., Commisso, C. E., & Austin, S. C. (2020). Multi-tiered systems of support. In T. W. Farmer, M. C. Conroy, E. M. Z. Farmer, & K. S. Sutherland (Eds.), *Handbook of research on emotional and behavioral disorders* (pp. 200–213). Routledge.

Kirsten, N. (2020). A systematic research review of teachers' professional development as a policy instrument. *Educational Research Review, 31,* 1–13. https://doi.org/10.1016/j. edurev.2020.100366

Knight, M., & Cooper, R. (2019). Taking on a new grading system: The interconnected effects of standards-based grading on teaching, learning, assessment, and student behavior. *NASSP Bulletin, 103*(1), 65–92.

Korpershoek, H., Harms, T., de Boer, H., van Kuijk, M., & Doolaard, S. (2016). A meta-analysis of the effects of classroom management strategies and classroom management programs on students' academic, behavioral, emotional, and motivational outcomes. *Review of Educational Research, 86*(3), 643–680.

Kyndt, E., Gijbels, D., Grosemans, I., & Donche, V. (2016). Teachers' everyday professional development: Mapping informal learning activities, antecedents, and learning outcomes. *Review of Educational Research, 86*(4), 1111–1150.

Lane, K. L., Buckman, M. M., Peia Oakes, W., & Menzies, H. (2020). Chapter 5: Tiered systems and inclusion: Potential benefits, clarifications, and considerations. In J. M. Kauffman (Ed.), *On educational inclusion: Meanings, history, issues and international perspectives.* Routledge.

Lewthwaite, B., Osborne, B., Lloyd, N., Boon, H., Llewellyn, L., Webber, T., Laffin, G., Harrison, M., Day, C., Kemp, C., & Wills, J. (2015). Seeking a pedagogy of difference: What Aboriginal students and their parents in North Queensland say about teaching and their learning. *Australian Journal of Teacher Education, 40*(5), 132–159.

Luke, A., Cazden, C., Coopes, R., Klenowski, V., Ladwig, J., Lester, J., Phillips, J., Shield, P., Spina, N., Theroux, P., Tones, M., Villegas, M., & Woods, A. (2013). *A summative evaluation of the stronger smarter learning communities project: 2013 report* (Vols. 1–2). Queensland University of Technology. https://eprints.qut.edu.au/59535/

Mahmud, A., & Satchell, L. (Eds.). (2022). *Mental wellbeing in schools: What teachers need to know to support pupils from diverse backgrounds.* Routledge. www.routledge. com/Mental-Wellbeing-in-Schools-What-Teachers-Need-to-Know-to-Support-Pupils/ Mahmud-Satchell/p/book/9780367749651

Mahoney, M. (2020). Implementing evidence-based practices within multi-Tiered systems of support to promote inclusive secondary classroom settings. *Journal of Special Education Apprenticeship, 9*(1), 10–12.

Mitchell, D. (2020). *What really works in special and inclusive education: Using evidence-based teaching strategies* (3rd ed.). Routledge.

Moodie, N. (2019). Learning about knowledge: Threshold concepts for Indigenous studies in education. *The Australian Educational Researcher, 46*(5), 735–749.

O'Meara, N., & Faulkner, F. (2021). Professional development for out-of-field post-primary teachers of mathematics: An analysis of the impact of mathematics specific pedagogy training. *Irish Educational Studies,* 1–20. https://doi.org/10.1080/03323315.2021.1899026

O'Neill, S., & Stephenson, J. (2014). Evidence-based classroom and behaviour management content in Australian pre-service primary teachers' coursework: Wherefore art thou? *Australian Journal of Teacher Education, 39*(4), 1–22. https://files.eric.ed.gov/fulltext/ EJ1017652.pdf

Paramita, P. P., Sharma, U., & Anderson, A. (2020). Effective teacher professional learning on classroom behaviour management: A review of literature. *Australian Journal of Teacher Education, 45*(1), 61–81.

Phillips, J. (2021). Foundations of teacher knowledge. In M. Shay & R. Oliver (Eds.), *Indigenous education in Australia: Learning and teaching for deadly futures* (pp. 7–20). Routledge.

Poed, S., Cowan, I., & Swain, N. (2020). *The high impact engagement strategies (HIES)*. Parkville College, Victorian Department of Education and Training. https://static1.squarespace.com/static/5977deef8419c27557b25893/t/5f488136fb21f8604a1 56a71/1598587217353/The%2BHighImpactEngagementStrategies%2BV4.0%2BF inal.pdf

Poed, S., & de Bruin, K. (2022). Chapter 4: Tier 2: Targeted approaches, interventions, and supports. In K. Barker, P. Whitefield, & S. Poed (Eds.), *School-wide positive behaviour support: The Australian handbook*. Routledge.

Richardson, R. (1998). Inclusive societies, inclusive schools – the terms of debate and action. *Multicultural Teaching, 16*(2), 23–29. https://eric.ed.gov/?id=EJ566945

Schulz, S., Morrison, A., Blanch, F., Buckskin, J., & Corrie, S. (2023). *Improving schooling and outcomes for Aboriginal and Torres Strait Islander learners in South Australian Catholic schools and centres: A narrative review of the literature*. The University of Adelaide and Flinders University.

Scruggs, T. E., & Mastropieri, M. A. (2002). On babies and bathwater: Addressing the problems of identification of learning disabilities. *Learning Disability Quarterly, 25*(3), 155–168.

Sharma, U. (2018). Preparing to teach in inclusive classrooms. In G. W. Noblit (Ed.), *Oxford research encyclopedia of education* (pp. 1–12). Oxford University Press. https://doi.org/10.1093/acrefore/9780190264093.013.113

Shay, M., & Miller, J. (2021). Excellence in indigenous education. In K. A. Allen, A. Reupert, & L. Oades (Eds.), *Building better schools with evidence-based policy* (pp. 46–54). Routledge.

Shay, M., & Oliver, R. (Eds.). (2021). *Indigenous education in Australia: Learning and teaching for deadly futures*. Routledge.

Tabach, M., & Trgalová, J. (2019). The knowledge and skills that mathematics teachers need for ICT integration: The issue of Standards. In G. Aldon & J. Trgalová (Eds.), *Technology in mathematics teaching* (pp. 183–203). Springer.

Telfer, S. L. (2020). *Effects of a within-school coaching model on teachers' use of behavioural feedback and opportunities to respond* [Doctoral dissertation, Murdoch University]. https://researchrepository.murdoch.edu.au/id/eprint/59275/

Thomas, C. (2020). *Inclusive schools build inclusive societies*. Brookings Institution. Retrieved November 6, 2023, from https://policycommons.net/artifacts/4139087/inclusive-schools-build-inclusive-societies/4947741/ CID: 20.500.12592/8r6kzk.

United Nations. (2015). *Sustainable development goals*. https://sdgs.un.org/goals#history

Vangrieken, K., Meredith, C., Packer, T., & Kyndt, E. (2017). Teacher communities as a context for professional development: A systematic review. *Teaching and Teacher Education, 61*, 47–59.

Victorian Department of Education and Training. (2020). *High impact teaching strategies* (Rev. ed.). Victorian Government. www.education.vic.gov.au/Documents/school/teachers/support/high-impact-teaching-strategies.pdf

Visible Learning. (2017). *Collective teacher efficacy (CTE) according to John Hattie*. https://visible-learning.org/2018/03/collective-teacher-efficacy-hattie/

Weldon, P. R. (2016). *Policy insights: Out-of-field teaching in Australian secondary schools*. Australian Council for Educational Research. https://research.acer.edu.au/policyinsights/6/

4 Educational leadership

Leading for learning

4.1 Introduction

Chapter 4 emphasises issues of educational leadership and highlights the role of leadership in enhancing student learning and engagement. The chapter provides preliminary insights into the nature of various meta-analyses that have sought to identify the characteristics of educational leadership practices that enhance student learning. At the same time, it also cautions against placing too much emphasis on such meta-analyses because they strip away necessary attention to context. In this vein, the chapter outlines how there is a need for greater inclusivity to ensure enhanced educational outcomes are more equitably distributed across the population. At the same time, the chapter also advocates for a more globally minded approach to leadership practices, given increasingly mobile and cosmopolitan populations in individual schooling systems around the world. The chapter also provides insights into the importance of managing the administrative burden upon principals and how identity, agency, and autonomy are critical for building sustainable leadership practices.

This chapter is premised on the following ideals:

- That school leadership is important in regards to school improvement and the lifting of student outcomes;
- Complexity of social issues impacts the daily operations taking place in schools, and the need for educational leaders to be

  - aware of and responsive to the social complexities of schooling and
  - Inclusive of local community needs;

- That educational leadership is located at all levels within a school (for example, teachers) and does not simply reside with principals or members of the executive leadership team;
- That educational leaders need to be supported in order to help them face the complexities of school leadership, and this is central to the wellbeing of educational leaders.

DOI: 10.4324/9781032666839-4

The provision of equitable and inclusive education at scale has been an enduring issue for governments, school systems, and schools. Of all the within-school factors contributing to equitable and inclusive outcomes, educational leadership has been identified as the second most influential behind classroom teaching (Leithwood et al., 2020). As a result, educational leadership is seen as a key policy lever for school and systemic reform targeted at improving school outcomes.

The central questions are, therefore, the following:

1. How can leadership be enacted to positively impact student outcomes?
2. How can schools and school systems productively support the development and ongoing performance of school leaders?

Addressing such questions requires nuanced understanding about what can be extrapolated from different kinds of research evidence, and the limitations of evidence types.

4.2   Looking at and beyond meta-analyses and systematic reviews

Within the educational leadership space, there has been considerable attention to various meta-analyses of existing educational leadership strategies/models or approaches that have been considered most impactful or effective. While attention to such studies is understandable to develop broad insights into educational leadership practices that may prove beneficial in different contexts, it is also important to move beyond a focus on meta-analyses alone since there are many other forms of research evidence within the field of educational leadership research. Focusing predominantly on one type (meta-analyses) misses the richness of detail and nuance provided by other types of research evidence. This is important to point out, especially if there is a desire to understand the complexities of leadership, such as how social issues impact daily operations. Meta-analyses often, inadvertently, wash out contextually relevant detail. As such, it is important to view many different kinds of evidence and not just rely on some types only. We consequently work from the premise that a broader range of educational leadership evidence can be very productive for enhancing practice.

Some large-scale meta-analyses and systematic syntheses have been conducted in and about educational leadership, with mixed outcomes. Since Robinson et al. (2008), this larger scale kind of analysis has become more common in educational leadership, but these analyses have caveats, which are important to point out.

Some meta-analyses have tried to analyse which kind of educational leadership styles (for example, transformational, distributed, instructional) are most effective for improving student outcomes, with mixed results (see Karadağ et al., 2015; Leithwood & Sun, 2012). This is not surprising given that: (1) educational leaders are not just principals and; (2) principals tend to exhibit more than just one-dimensional features when doing their work in schools. For example, principals may need to exhibit some elements of transformational leadership in order to develop instructional leadership. Trying to isolate a 'type' of leadership is not really that helpful when acknowledging the complexity of schools and the myriad challenges they face. Similarly, educational leaders can be found at all levels within a school environment, so trying to isolate just the work of principals is perhaps an outdated way of conceiving where leadership can be, and often is, located within schools.

Other meta-analyses have tried to analyse the degree of impact that school leaders have on improving student achievement (see Karadağ, 2020; Wu & Shen, 2022; Liebowitz & Porter, 2019). While educational leadership is generally considered to have a positive effect on student achievement, it must be noted that: (1) such leadership goes beyond those in formal leadership roles and; (2) context matters. Thus, Wu and Shen (2022) argue for the need to seek out further kinds of evidence.

Alongside these meta studies, there have also been some mega-analyses (a step beyond meta) in education more generally that discuss educational leadership (see Hattie, 2009). While popular within the public domain, there is (and has been for some time) a growing body of research that critiques the claims being made by these broader studies (e.g. Bergeron & Rivard, 2017; Higgins, 2016). One of the more popular criticisms relates to methodology. Meta-analyses are reliant on the quality of the variables entered into the analysis. In other words, what is classified and how variables are defined, really matter, and if how a variable is defined is questionable (or lacks transparency), then that severely impacts the effects of the variables being claimed (Higgins, 2016, pp. 37–40). Moreover, how to ascertain what can and cannot be classified as having an effect is also really important. Snook et al. (2009) explain this well. Understanding the limitations and parameters of extrapolation from a large meta-analysis (or any kind of research) is really important, so it is vital to avoid solely relying on this kind of research evidence.

Systematic reviews have also become an increasingly popular way of trying to capture the existing knowledge base of leadership and its effect on student outcomes as well. As with meta-analyses, there are multiple types including those aimed at the entire field (Gumus et al., 2018; Hallinger, 2014; Hitt & Tucker, 2016) and those targeting specific geographic regions (Hallinger & Chen, 2015; Hammad et al., 2022). Systematic reviews, like meta- and/or mega-analyses, are also dependent on the information entered into the review. Transparency is key.

One recent systematic review of principal (not school leaders more broadly) effects on students and schools is provided by Grissom et al. (2021). This commissioned report was published by the Wallace Foundation. Using a set of transparent criteria, Grissom et al. (2021) argue that there are

> four principal practices that are linked to effective outcomes, as well as three foundational skills. The four practices, which together provide a rounded portrait of principal activities, are high-leverage instructional activities, building a productive culture and climate, facilitating collaboration and learning communities, and the strategic management of personnel and resources.

> (p. x)

Importantly, this report emphasises and overlays the need for equity given the changing and challenging social contexts within which schools are located. This recognition of the complex and diverse nature of schooling is why it has been flagged. It resonates with the desire to embrace, acknowledge, and act upon diversity. It is one of the few larger scale reports that take issues of equity into explicit consideration.

It is problematic to try to generalise which educational leadership types and practices are most effective in improving school outcomes because schools vary, and these prescriptive approaches ignore the specificities of context. What works in one school may not work in another. Even within the same school, there may be a need to approach various issues differently. International research (Ribbins & Gronn, 2013) (including research in the Australian context [Kamara, 2017]) emphasises the need to see educational leadership as a socially bounded process. In short, context matters. School leaders need to be encouraged to shape their practices according to the specific conditions within their school. There is consequently a substantial body of literature (see Niesche & Gowlett, 2019, pp. 1–3) critiquing 'best practice' models of educational leadership, and it is important to take such critiques into account to nuance understandings of the potential benefits of these broader studies.

Key message: There are meta-analyses that try to ascertain the most impactful and effective leadership strategies, but relying solely on them is problematic. They are mostly useful for making the general claim that educational leadership has a positive effect on school and student outcomes. Caution should, however, be taken when deciding which ones to draw upon. Understanding the parameters of their usability is paramount.

Ways forward: Instead of asking which leadership models and practices are most effective and impactful for school and student improvement, it is perhaps more useful to instead ask: How can school leadership positively influence student learning? With this question, there is a much larger variety of research literature and evidence – particularly context-sensitive/relevant material – upon which to draw.

4.3 How can leadership be enacted to positively shape student outcomes?

4.3.1 *Focusing on inclusivity, equity, and social justice*

It is well known that schools in many countries provide high-quality education overall but need a lot of work in terms of equity. Consequently, there is a (growing) body of educational leadership research focused on social justice, and how this can be attained (Wilkinson et al., 2018). Educational inequality is a major issue needing to be addressed in schooling, and school leaders play a vital role in remedying this situation.

Educational leadership plays a critical role in fostering the inclusion of young people situated on the margins of schooling. Equity is not simply about educational leaders improving the *outcomes* of those disengaged from schooling. While outcomes are important, it is the *processes* educational leaders use to work with local community members that really matter and that need attention (Hameed et al., 2021). For example, in the Australian context, attaining excellence in Aboriginal and Torres Strait Islander education necessitates development of productive relations between peoples, specifically 'authentic, purposeful and relationally based engagement between institutions and Aboriginal communities' (The Australian TAFE Teacher, 2018). *How* educational leaders go about engaging with community is crucial, and it is dependent on the local context (Shay & Lampert, 2022). School leaders need to be aware of this. They need to be aware of working with their local community in a respectful way, valuing local knowledge and authentically listening to issues of concern. Inclusive leadership (involving school leaders, teacher leaders, community leaders) entails adopting a strengths-based approach when supporting Indigenous students, embedding Indigenous knowledges and perspectives, and supporting the wellbeing of Indigenous students (Shay et al., 2021). Supportive and inclusive leadership is thus about empowering students to have a strong and positive sense of self.

An underlying aspect of inclusive leadership, as mentioned, is about equitable access and this ethos is manifested through culturally responsive practices meeting the needs of a diversified student demographic. With leadership theories becoming more inclusive and integrative, there is an emphasis on 'multiple dimensions of individual identities and context, organisational cultures and subcultures, visions for transformational change, and ethical principles' (Eagly & Chin, 2010, p. 221). Scholars have highlighted that there is a close connection between students' cultural background, effective instruction and improved learning. Indeed, '[a] substantial number of studies have shown that when local knowledge plays a dominant role in instruction (usually in combination with use of the Native language), improvements are seen in various performance and attainment measures' (Demmert, 2001, p. 19; also see Castagno & Brayboy, 2008).

The earlier works of Ladson-Billings (1995) on teachers' cultural reference to both pedagogy and classroom management (Weinstein et al., 2004) have been expanded to the Indigenous field (Castagno & Brayboy, 2008). It is important to note that there are multiple dimensions to consider when transforming educational institutions into cultural enterprises and they include policy reforms, administrative processes and funding (Gay, 2013), and most importantly, the role of school leadership in this reformation process (Khalifa et al., 2016). Culturally responsive leadership is an all-encompassing model that targets practices at multiple levels and within varying contexts – from school leaders to teacher leaders (Villegas & Lucas, 2002), to district-level leaders (Castagno & Brayboy, 2008), and to community leaders (Khalifa, 2012). Such leadership focuses on relationship building with community, leads professional development opportunities for teachers and staff, and most importantly, adopts culturally responsive practices across the whole school setting (Khalifa et al., 2016).

With reference to Indigenous education, it is critical to focus on professional practice and engagement to better equip teachers with pedagogical knowledge and skills that support and engage with young people from Indigenous communities (Brown, 2019). Teachers need to be supported in their professional learning and culturally responsive development (AITSL, 2022). Bodkin-Andrews et al. (2021) proposes strategies and methods that educators in Australian schools can harness to support Aboriginal and Torres Strait Islander students in their classrooms. These include the provision of alternative ways of discussing and promoting respectful conversations on issues such as race and racism, and intervention strategies when racism is witnessed (Bodkin-Andrews et al., 2021). There is also a need to develop co-constructed pedagogies for Aboriginal and Torres Strait Islander learners that includes engagement with students, teachers and community (Armour & Miller, 2021).

4.3.2 *Being globally minded in a changing cosmopolitan landscape*

Scholars in the field of leadership also maintain the importance of leaders being globally minded, appreciative of cultural diversity and aware of the need to build affiliations across cultural divides (Gaudelli, 2014; Hameed, 2020; Hargreaves & Shirley, 2012). This is aligned with the idea of possessing a 'cosmopolitan disposition.' According to Rizvi (2008, 2012), a cosmopolitan disposition enables an individual to understand local issues within a broader context of global change – change that is responsible for the restructuring of local contexts and environments, including social identities. Cosmopolitanism places high importance on the effects of globalisation, worldviews, and cultural inclusivity (Vongalis-Macrow, 2009). Importantly, having a cosmopolitan disposition allows leaders to understand eclectic educational landscapes – both within individual schools and beyond – as diverse and rich. This is critical as a means of facilitating inclusion.

In contrast, an ethnocentric disposition (which is to be avoided) encourages a judgement of cultures according to preconceptions originating in customs and ideas from one's own culture, and which lends itself to cultural bias and discrimination. In the context of schooling and educational leadership, ethnocentrism thus lends itself to marginalising students who bring different cultural understandings to school (Hameed, 2022). Twenty-first century leaders need to be those that possess a cosmopolitan mindset, leaders who are conscious of ethics and cosmopolitan accountabilities within a diversified, inclusive, interconnected and complex globalised world (Hameed, 2022). Furthermore, '[a]s leadership theories become more inclusive and integrative, they have more potential to take into account multiple dimensions of individual identities and context, organizational cultures and subcultures . . . visions for transformational change, and ethical principles' (Eagly & Chin, 2010, p. 221). It is thus critical for leaders to be globally minded, appreciate cultural diversity and inclusivity, and build affiliations across cultural divides (Gaudelli, 2014; Hargreaves & Shirley, 2012). A recent study by Hameed (2022) showed that school leaders' 'cosmopolitan leadership' disposition helped them drive the global citizenship agenda in their respective schools:

> School leaders were influential in driving and determining the type of education that the students received, as a result of their cosmopolitan disposition nurtured by their global experiences. Their individual cultural capital as a result of their global experiences, as well as their outward-looking dispositions, were integral in shaping some of the policies and initiatives around global citizenship education.
>
> (p. 86)

The type of education that students currently attain in schools should facilitate intercultural understanding and confer an international outlook, as this will enable students to have a better understanding of the diverse, multifaceted nature of the globalised environment in which they live and study (Rizvi, 2008). School leaders consequently need to provide a learning environment conducive to the development and recognition of a diversified student population in order to meet the challenges of an increasingly interconnected and mobile 21st-century population. Understanding leadership from a broader dimension includes an investigation into the behavioural dispositions, attitudes, values, outlook, and theory that covers a range of adaptable characteristics (Zeller, 2015).

Whilst a global outlook is important, there is an intricate relationship between local and global aspects (Rizvi & Lingard, 2010), which is sometimes referred to as a 'global-local nexus' (Edwards & Usher, 2008, p. 22). In the discussion of leadership in the current landscape, it is important to acknowledge the impact of the global and the local nexus on leadership principles and ways of influence that come about because of such global – local influence (Stobie, 2016). It is also important to understand the symbiotic relationship between the national and the global which is fundamental to the various theorisations within the cosmopolitan turn (Hameed, 2020).

According to Cohen (2010), a global mindset is 'the ability to think and act both locally and globally at the same time' (p. 5). Under such circumstances, 'leaders need to understand the facts about different countries, cultures, and business procedures, as well as local information about customs and practices, both from a social and business perspective' (Cohen, 2010, p. 28).

4.3.3   *Harnessing the leadership potential of teachers*

Fostering the leadership capabilities of teachers is without doubt a critical aspect of school leadership. Researchers have agreed that not only principals but teachers can lead schools and positively influence instructional practices by sharing their knowledge and practices and working collaboratively. The development of the leadership capacities of teachers contributes to the overall capacity of the school, leading to better educational outcomes. Accordingly, teacher leadership (TL) has recently received increasing attention in contexts where improving students' performance is a prominent concern (Wenner & Campbell, 2017).

TL has been used as an umbrella term to describe an array of different tasks teachers do beyond classroom teaching, associated with, for example, supporting the professional development of their peers and getting involved in decision-making processes (Wenner & Campbell, 2017). That is to say, there is no clear consensus about what tasks teacher leaders are expected to take on. Indeed, considering that leading 'exists only through its manifestations' (Hopkins & Jackson, 2002), it is natural that teachers' leading practices can take on many different forms in different schools.

Furthermore, a deeper understanding of TL should not merely focus on what (specific tasks) teachers do but rather, the conditions under which TL is more likely to flourish and positively impact students' schooling experiences. First, TL requires teachers to engage in some sort of formal or informal training so that they develop the knowledge and skills they need to take on leadership tasks. Alongside such training, there are also factors that either facilitate or constrain the actual implementation of teacher leadership. Drawing on the latest literature review conducted by Wenner and Campbell (2017), research on TL suggests principals play a critical role in shaping such factors. On the one hand, principals must be willing to share their authority and power and distribute leadership tasks to teachers. However, caution is raised that exercising TL may be misinterpreted as the simple delegation of extra tasks to teachers, which may have negative implications for teachers' wellbeing through the increase in what may be an already heavy workload. Consequently, delegation of leaders' tasks to teachers must be coupled with a school environment that takes teachers' work into account. In this regard, research suggests that for the successful implementation of TL, principals need to engage in both logistical and cultural work within schools in order to set clear, well-defined tasks for teachers, provide flexible schedules, and create a school climate in which teachers feel trusted, valued, and empowered to take risks (Wenner & Campbell, 2017).

Notably, the development and growth of leadership capabilities is intrinsically related to empowerment, opportunity, and space (Hopkins & Jackson, 2002). In line with this, TL should not be understood as simply the distribution of tasks to teachers but the enhancement of teachers' instructional capabilities through the creation of spaces and opportunities where teachers can exercise autonomy, creativity, collaboration, and reflection on their work and share it with others. In other words, building leadership capacity is about creating opportunities and the appropriate environment for learning (Harris & Lambert, 2003). If teachers can exercise TL under appropriate conditions, it may benefit teachers and schools by increasing their leadership and instructional capacity and improve teachers' levels of self-confidence and professional satisfaction. In contrast, if schools experience a lack of strong-trusting relationships, effective communication, ethics of care, and clear goals and responsibilities, attempts to implement TL may lead teachers to suffer stress and burnout and damage their relationships with their peers (Wenner & Campbell, 2017).

Key message: The demography of students is increasingly diverse, eclectic, and evolving. Educational leaders must consequently focus on inclusivity and embrace cosmopolitanism. Harnessing the leadership potential of teachers is pivotal to such work.

Ways forward: Supporting educational leaders is essential. This includes examining *how* schools and school systems can support teachers to take on educational leadership roles in ways that enhance and highlight their practice and that of their colleagues.

4.4 What are other forms of relevant educational leadership research telling us?

4.4.1 The administrative work of school principals

School-based management has significantly increased the administrative work of school principals. The intensification of school principals' responsibilities not only negatively impacts principals' perception of their job but also the overall performance of the school as it steers the attention of educators away from teaching and learning. Data from the Organisation for Economic Cooperation and Development (OECD) (2019) *Teaching and Learning International Survey* (TALIS) indicates that, for example, Australian school leaders spend as little as 11% of their time on teaching and learning related activities. This is below OECD (2019) averages. Principals having discretion to make local decisions is not so much of a concern. Instead, it is the substantial increase in administrative tasks that needs to be taken into account. As Gonski et al. (2018) point out:

Giving schools autonomy over decisions, in the right context, and over the right things, can improve school performance. It can, however, also increase the administrative burden as administrative tasks that were previously undertaken centrally are devolved to school leaders. Principals in most systems exercise greater local discretion than a decade ago, but the amount of information required by the system about the management of the school has also increased.

(p. 85)

In other words, school principals are, in many ways, required to undertake more and more administration, which prevents them from being able to productively engage in innovative leadership focused on teaching and learning. A survey of secondary school teachers across Australia, conducted by Heffernan and Pierpoint (2020), is extremely useful for understanding what 'administrivia' means in the current context. The survey responses indicate that school-based accountability is burdening principals with pressures that far exceed an education focus – like building maintenance and capital works – tasks that were previously managed centrally. Australian primary school principals report similar frustrations in a nationwide survey titled *Out of Balance* (Australian Primary Principals' Association [APPA], 2017). This report reveals that workload is becoming less focused on teaching and learning and more focused on administration issues that could (and were previously) managed centrally. In APPA's (2017) survey response, the example of a tree audit is used to highlight how principals' work has become disproportionately focused on tasks that could be (and were) conducted by central education departments. These surveys provide valuable insight into how the work of principals has shifted from teaching and learning, without sufficient support and guidance from district and central offices, thus resulting in principal burnout. Moreover, heavy workload has been found to be an important barrier to job satisfaction in many countries (Schleicher & OECD, 2012), leading to concerns about principal retention as a key issue.

The solution is not to take away local discretion; such discretion is central to enacting substantive educational leadership. Instead, the working conditions of school principals can be improved by better (re)defining their roles (Heffernan & Pierpoint, 2020) as well as formulating sensible responsibilities and boundaries so that their work can be made more feasible. Similarly, there is a need to assist principals with this administrative workload, which can then free them up to undertake more teaching and learning focused leadership activities and associated cultural change.

4.4.2   *Leadership identity, agency, and autonomy as critical*

Leadership development goes far beyond just understanding the principles and types of leadership. Leadership development focuses upon the importance of cultivating three areas – *leadership identity* (e.g. Day & Harrison, 2007; DeRue & Ashford, 2010), *leadership agency* (Day & Dragoni, 2015; Rosch & Villanueva, 2016), and *leadership autonomy* – all of which are essential for addressing issues of diversity, equity, and inclusion. These are considered essential concerns for developing effective 21st-century leaders (Cundiff et al., 2018; Dugan, 2017). There is thus a body of literature that advocates for shifting away from leadership models to instead focusing more on the developmental process of leadership (Day et al., 2014).

In unpacking *leadership identity*, it is critical to know that leadership identity is not just an intrapersonal trait nor one-directional or static in form. Instead, leadership identity is dynamic and relational. It encompasses various contextual factors resulting in many shifts over a period of time and across different situations; in particular, leaders' identities shift through social construction (DeRue & Ashford, 2010). Identity formation in essence centres around the motivations and the moral purpose of an individual. It highlights clarity of purpose, one's conviction towards a visionary goal and a willingness to position oneself based on defined values shaping identity. The development of leadership identities assists in better understanding relational outcomes. Researchers in the field have recognised the key role that identity plays in the support of personal growth (Day & Dragoni, 2015; Day et al., 2014; Day & Harrison, 2007).

Leadership autonomy and agency are interwoven with school leaders' efforts to address issues within their schools. They form the heart of 'knowing and doing' within an organisation. Leadership autonomy and agency strip away the bureaucratic governance that hinders the improvement of existing systems. Through agency, leaders are given voices to restructure dominant discourses, overcome structural hurdles, and collaboratively engage with key stakeholders in attaining the desired goals of the organisation. Such agency enables leaders to be both competent and proactive. With school autonomy and leadership, there is a focus on innovation and effective use of resources (Keddie, 2016). Autonomy provides the opportunity for ingenuity, but at the same time, judgement is key to deciding on which domains to address at any given moment within schools. This includes knowing when to question norms and how to assist both system and school personnel who may be challenged by such questioning. The focus of such reforms, most importantly, is not solely on academic achievement ascertained by narrow performance measures but instead upon student engagement and the pursuit of equity and citizenship goals – which are all associated with a moral leadership sensibility (Fullan, 2002, 2020).

4.4.3 Supporting flexible rather than prescriptive accountability

Current accountability systems place great emphasis on performance (e.g. standardised test results) assuming that this is the path towards improvement. Taking assessment performance as the main indicator of the quality of schools and school leadership has fostered competition and comparison among schools, placing significant pressure on school leaders and, arguably, shifting the purpose of schooling. Moreover, this narrow approach to accountability leaves other important aspects and educational stakeholders out of the picture, marginalising more holistic, multi-directional approaches and more varied, contextually relevant, 'authentic' accountabilities (Hardy, 2021).

More traditional and standardised assessment performance does not account for the educational processes individual schools undertake in response to the particular needs of their local communities. Therefore, there is an emerging call for policymakers to acknowledge that effective educational leadership needs to be understood within the context of the school and the issues it is facing. Eacott (2018a, 2022) argues that there is a need to flip how we see and enact accountability for school principals, shifting it away from measures outside of the school's local context, to instead being generated by principals in regard to their own specific school needs and conditions. This means principals should (1) create a clarity of purpose focused on their school sites, (2) be judged on their level of coherence against that purpose, and (3) construct a narrative for their school concerning how they will, and are, moving towards their goals (Eacott, 2018a). This type of relational approach to leadership accountability encourages leaders to be context-driven whilst still retaining accountability. This approach also has the potential to better address the needs of students and educators and community in regional, rural, and remote school settings (Eacott et al., 2021). A context-driven, relational approach to leadership ensures flexibility and adaptability to meet the needs of the community (Eacott, 2018b). Such targeted goals and vision are able to capture a school's key priorities and challenges.

An important point to note is that relationality also centres on issues of equity and inclusion (Shields, 2018). An inclusive school community ensures that all students' needs are addressed as well as systemic inequities. This helps foster culturally responsive leadership (as outlined earlier). In summary, a context-driven, relationally attuned leadership approach enables principals to foster school environments that are equitable, responsive, and innovative.

Relatedly, developing more 'internal' forms of accountability allows schools to identify, address, and communicate about meaningful learning, aspects that hinder the achievement of their goals, and educational opportunities (Lingard et al., 2017). In other words, through the internal accountability practices of schools, a more comprehensive account of the different domains and actors impacting education can be developed. Such an approach consequently expands the range of indicators of good education and school leadership. Such internal accountability systems (managed by schools), combined with external accountability processes (managed by school systems), enable more democratic forms of accountability in which not only educators but also governments and communities are held responsible for education (Lingard et al., 2017).

4.4.4   *Response-able leadership means giving due concern to non-human entities*

A much newer field of educational leadership research focuses on the material and non-human aspects of schooling. Anthropocentrism – the idea that human beings are the most important or sole entity to consider – is no longer acceptable within this branch of thinking. Arguably, we are living in what has been described as the post-Anthropocene, which sees humans as importantly entangled with non-human entities, such as the environment, animals, and technology. This has implications for *thinking* about educational leadership. It has implications for *doing* educational leadership and, importantly, *being* an educational leader. This may be an uncomfortable shift in thinking for some people, but in this section, we invite you to temporarily suspend judgement while we explain.

Non-human 'things' are important. We know this when thinking about the organisation of a classroom. How it is organised shapes the sense of place and belonging that all who enter into it feel. The organisation of inanimate things in the classroom has the power to include and exclude. We thus know that non-human things do matter in education. Think about this at the everyday level. When school leaders are making decisions about technology, such decisions have a profound impact that transcends the people (students and teachers) who will be using such technology. The expected life span of the devices purchased for a school has implications for the environment, with technological waste rising at an exponentially high rate. Anthropocentric leadership – leadership which thinks about only the human without considering its entanglement with other non-human entities – is an outdated form of educational leadership. In contrast, a post-anthropocentric educational leadership is one imbued with an ethics of care. This includes care for the inanimate and how decision-making around inanimate objects and entities shape human experience, and vice versa.

Post-anthropocentric leadership requires us to understand the forcefulness of inanimate things in shaping educational practices. As Niesche and Gowlett (2019) outline:

> Humans-as-leaders have a long and strongly entrenched history within this field of research, but perhaps, it is timely to de-centre [humans-as-leaders] from our analyses and draw more attention to the non-human and its constituting capabilities. Shifting the idea of matter from a noun to a verb certainly requires some intellectual mind bending, since the passivity of matter has a 'common-sense' appeal. However, so too does the liveliness of matter when we talk about the effects that data, emails and policy have on the formation of school and leadership success. One need only think about the force of an email in their inbox (or multiple emails in their inbox!) and the feelings that this can invoke, to also 'see' the common-sense appeal of giving matter its deserved recognition in meaning-making – its vitality and force in shaping what counts.
>
> (p. 129)

If educational leadership is formed through the entanglement of both human and non-human entities, then alteration and change are consequently garnered through a reconfiguration of that entanglement. This is where an ethics of care comes into play.

Thinking about the non-human in a 'response-able' (Barad, 2012) way is how this reconfiguration can occur. It is how productive change can happen. This means stopping to think deeply about how to respond and what this might look like. With the examples listed so far, this could mean rethinking the purchasing of technology equipment so that it minimises environmental impact (which may mean not just purchasing what is least expensive). With the forcefulness of performance data, it could mean deconstructing the effects (and often discriminatory power) of algorithmic information and instead turning toward more contextual and meaningful student information (not just test results but other forms of evidence of student learning). With schooling infrastructure and design, such an approach entails thinking about the environmental and ecological impact, along with where items are being sourced from (seeking to minimise the carbon footprint and helping local businesses). Response-able educational leadership is all about reconfiguring the conversation about what matters by paying attention to the other-than-human things that have force in shaping educational outcomes and society in general. We flag this emerging school of thinking about educational leadership because it provides a new and exciting way to think differently about what educational leadership may look like, be, and focus on.

Key message: Principals are reporting being taken away from teaching and learning focused leadership by administrative tasks that were previously managed by district and central offices (e.g. capital works, tree audits). They are also reporting high rates of burnout and excessive work stress, with principal retention being positioned as a key problem moving forward. Finding a way for principals to focus on issues relating to teaching and learning is essential.

Ways forward: Productive leadership builds respectful relationships with the community and the local environment. Principals consequently require authority to make context-specific decisions that work best for their students, staff, and the broader school community. Principals require administrative support with tasks not focused on teaching and learning. There is also a need for increased flexibility to innovate in the space of teaching and learning. This desire to innovate is possible without sacrificing accountability. Being response-able is key to this, including in relation to the broader environment in which schooling is undertaken.

4.5   Conclusion

Educational leadership is complex but productive leadership is also very achievable. This requires the capacity not only to apply broad principles to local contexts where relevant but also to actively recognise and support those practices at the local level that are generative of teacher and student learning. This necessitates a more strengths-based approach to recognising leadership and educational potential more broadly. Leadership resides in a variety of places within a school, and recognising this is important. Addressing the requirements of an increasingly diverse, more cosmopolitan student body is essential. Understanding the importance of human leadership being entangled with non-human entities is also crucial. Attention to supporting principals' agency and autonomy are key to the sorts of flexible accountabilities that are likely to lead to more substantive system, school, and, ultimately, student learning. Leading *for* learning is central to effective, productive, and inclusive educational leadership.

4.6   Chapter questions

1. What are the limitations to meta-analyses?
2. What kinds of evidence do you use to inform leadership decision-making in your context? How much is quantitative and how much is qualitative? Is there an appropriate balance?
3. What is cosmopolitanism, and how often does it factor into your leadership decision-making?
4. Take an audit of where your educational leadership time is being spent. Over the next week, track how you are spending your time. What tasks are you doing?

Does this reflect where you wish to spend your leadership time? What strategies can you implement within your school/system to ensure that you are enacting the kind of leadership that you value and that your school needs?

5. How much do you consider the non-human in your educational leadership decision-making? Provide examples of how you do and/or provide examples of how you could.

4.7 References

AITSL. 2022. *AITSL*. Retrieved November 16, from https://www.aitsl.edu.au/

Armour, D., & Miller, J. (2021). Relational pedagogies and co-constructing curriculum. In *Indigenous education in Australia* (pp. 162–173). Routledge.

Australian Primary Principals' Association. (2017). *Out of balance: The workload never stops. Preliminary report for the Adelaide symposium 2017*. Australian Primary Principals Association.

The Australian Tafe Teacher. (2018, Spring). Achieving excellence in Aboriginal and Torres Strait Islander education. *52*(3). www.aeufederal.org.au/download_file/view/1544/2435

Barad, K. (2012). Interview with Karen Barad. In I. Van der Tuin & R. Dolphijn (Eds.), *New materialism: Interview & cartographies* (pp. 48–70). Open Humanities Press.

Bergeron, P.-J., & Rivard, L. (2017). How to engage in pseudoscience with real data: A criticism of John Hattie's arguments in *visible learning* from the perspective of a statistician. *McGill Journal of Education/Revue des sciences de l'éducation de McGill*, *52*(1), 237–246.

Bodkin-Andrews, G., Foster, S., Bodkin, F., Foster, J., Andrews, G., Adams, K., & Evans, R. (2021). Resisting the racist silence: When racism and education collide. In *Indigenous education in Australia* (pp. 21–37). Routledge.

Brown, L. (2019). Indigenous young people, disadvantage and the violence of settler colonial education policy and curriculum. *Journal of Sociology*, *55*(1), 54–71.

Castagno, A. E., & Brayboy, B. M. J. (2008). Culturally responsive schooling for indigenous youth: A review of the literature. *Review of Educational Research*, *78*(4), 941–993.

Cohen, S. L. (2010). Effective global leadership requires a global mindset. *Industrial and Commercial Training*, *42*(1), 3–10.

Cundiff, J. L., Ryuk, S., & Cech, K. (2018). Identity-safe or threatening? Perceptions of women-targeted diversity initiatives. *Group Processes & Intergroup Relations*, *21*(5), 745–766.

Day, D. V., & Dragoni, L. (2015). Leadership development: An outcome-oriented review based on time and levels of analyses. *Annual Review of Organizational Psychology and Organizational Behavior*, *2*(1), 133–156.

Day, D. V., Fleenor, J. W., Atwater, L. E., Sturm, R. E., & McKee, R. A. (2014). Advances in leader and leadership development: A review of 25 years of research and theory. *The Leadership Quarterly*, *25*(1), 63–82.

Day, D. V., & Harrison, M. M. (2007). A multilevel, identity-based approach to leadership development. *Human Resource Management Review*, *17*(4), 360–373.

Demmert, W. G., Jr. (2001). *Improving academic performance among native American students: A review of the research literature*. Clearinghouse on Rural Education and Small Schools.

DeRue, D. S., & Ashford, S. J. (2010). Who will lead and who will follow? A social process of leadership identity construction in organizations. *Academy of Management Review*, *35*(4), 627–647.

Dugan, J. P. (2017). *Leadership theory: Cultivating critical perspectives*. John Wiley & Sons.

Eacott, S. (2018a). *Beyond leadership: A relational approach to organizational theory in education*. Springer.

Eacott, S. (2018b). Empowering educators through flipped school leadership. In D. M. Netolicky, J. Andrews, & C. Paterson (Eds.), *Flip the system Australia: What matters in education* (pp. 189–197). Taylor & Francis Group.

Eacott, S. (2022). The principals' workday: A relational analysis. *International Journal of Leadership in Education, 25*(2), 258–271.

Eacott, S., Niesche, R., Heffernan, A., Loughland, T., Gobby, B., & Durksen, T. (2021). *High-impact school leadership: Regional, rural and remote schools.* Commonwealth Department of Education, Skills and Employment.

Eagly, A. H., & Chin, J. L. (2010). Diversity and leadership in a changing world. *American Psychologist, 65*(3), 216.

Edwards, R., & Usher, R. (2008). *Globalisation and pedagogy: Space, place and identity* (2nd ed.). Routledge.

Fullan, M. (2002). The change. *Educational Leadership, 59*(8), 16–20.

Fullan, M. (2020). The nature of leadership is changing. *European Journal of Education, 55*(2), 139–142.

Gaudelli, W. (2014). *World class: Teaching and learning in global times.* Routledge.

Gay, G. (2013). Teaching to and through cultural diversity. *Curriculum Inquiry, 43*(1), 48–70.

Gonski, D., Arcus, T., Boston, K., Gould, V., Johnson, W., O'Brien, L., Perry, L. A., & Roberts, M. (2018). *Through growth to achievement: Report of the review to achieve educational excellence in Australian schools.* Commonwealth of Australia.

Grissom, J. A., Egalite, A. J., & Lindsay, C. A. (2021). *How principals affect students and schools: A systematic synthesis of two decades of research.* The Wallace Foundation.

Gumus, S., Bellibas, M. S., Esen, M., & Gumus, E. (2018). A systematic review of studies on leadership models in educational research from 1980 to 2014. *Educational Management Administration & Leadership, 46*(1), 25–48.

Hallinger, P. (2014). Reviewing reviews of research in educational leadership: An empirical assessment. *Educational Administration Quarterly, 50*(4), 539–576.

Hallinger, P., & Chen, J. (2015). Review of research on educational leadership and management in Asia: A comparative analysis of research topics and methods, 1995–2012. *Educational Management Administration & Leadership, 43*(1), 5–27.

Hameed, S. (2020). A comparative study of GCE and international curricula in Singapore and Australia. *International Journal of Educational Development, 78*, 102248.

Hameed, S. (2022). Cosmopolitan leadership in the institutionalization of global citizenship education: A comparative study of Singapore and Australia's practices. *Journal of School Leadership, 32*(1), 77–97.

Hameed, S., Shay, M., & Miller, J. (2021). 'Deadly leadership' in the pursuit of indigenous education excellence. *Future Alternatives for Educational Leadership: Diversity, Inclusion, Equity and Democracy*, 93–110.

Hammad, W., Samier, E. A., & Mohammed, A. (2022). Mapping the field of educational leadership and management in the Arabian Gulf region: A systematic review of Arabic research literature. *Educational Management Administration & Leadership, 50*(1), 6–25.

Hardy, I. (2021). *School reform in an era of standardization: Authentic accountabilities.* Routledge.

Hargreaves, A., & Shirley, D. L. (2012). *The global fourth way: The quest for educational excellence.* Corwin Press.

Harris, A., & Lambert, L. (2003). *Building leadership capacity for school improvement.* Open University Press.

Hattie, J. A. C. (2009). *Visible learning: A synthesis of over 800 meta-analyses relating to achievement.* Routledge.

Heffernan, A., & Pierpoint, A. (2020). *Autonomy, accountability, and principals' work: An Australian study.* Australian Secondary Principals' Association.

Higgins. (2016). Meta-synthesis and comparative meta-analysis of education research findings: Some risks and benefits. *Review of Education (Oxford), 4*(1), 31–53.

Hitt, D. H., & Tucker, P. D. (2016). Systematic review of key leader practices found to influence student achievement: A unified framework. *Review of Educational Research, 86*(2), 531–569.

Hopkins, D., & Jackson, D. (2002). Building the capacity for leading and learning. In A. Harris, C. Day, D. Hopkins, M. Hadfield, A. Hargreaves, & C. Chapman (Eds.), *Effective leadership for school improvement* (1st ed., pp. 84–104). Routledge.

Kamara, M. (2017). Remote and invisible: The voices of female Indigenous educational leaders in Northern Territory remote community schools in Australia. *Journal of Educational Administration and History, 49*(2), 128–143.

Karadağ, E. (2020). The effect of educational leadership on students' achievement: A cross-cultural meta-analysis research on studies between 2008 and 2018. *Asia Pacific Education Review, 21*(1), 49–64.

Karadağ, E., Bektaş, F., Çoğaltay, N., & Yalçın, M. (2015). The effect of educational leadership on students' achievement: A meta-analysis study. *Asia Pacific Education Review, 16*(1), 79–93.

Keddie, A. (2016). School autonomy as 'the way of the future' issues of equity, public purpose and moral leadership. *Educational Management Administration & Leadership, 44*(5), 713–727.

Khalifa, M. (2012). A re-new-ed paradigm in successful urban school leadership: Principal as community leader. *Educational Administration Quarterly, 48*(3), 424–467.

Khalifa, M. A., Gooden, M. A., & Davis, J. E. (2016). Culturally responsive school leadership: A synthesis of the literature. *Review of Educational Research, 86*(4), 1272–1311.

Ladson-Billings, G. (1995). Toward a theory of culturally relevant pedagogy. *American Educational Research Journal, 32*(3), 465–491.

Leithwood, K., Harris, A., & Hopkins, D. (2020). Seven strong claims about successful school leadership revisited. *School Leadership & Management, 40*(1), 5–22.

Leithwood, K., & Sun, J. (2012). The nature and effects of transformational school leadership: A meta-analytic review of unpublished research. *Educational Administration Quarterly, 48*(3), 387–423.

Liebowitz, D. D., & Porter, L. (2019). The effect of principal behaviors on student, teacher, and school outcomes: A systematic review and meta-analysis of the empirical literature. *Review of Educational Leadership Research, 89*(5), 785–827.

Lingard, B., Sellar, S., & Lewis, S. (2017). *Accountabilities in schools and school systems. Oxford research encyclopedia of education* (pp. 1–23). Oxford University Press. https://doi.org/10.1093/acrefore/9780190264093.013.74

Niesche, R., & Gowlett, C. (2019). *Social, critical and political theories for educational leadership*. Springer.

OECD. (2019). *TALIS 2018 results: Vol. 1. Teachers and school leaders as lifelong learners, TALIS*. OECD Publishing.

Ribbins, P., & Gronn, P. (2013). Researching principals: Context and culture in the study of leadership in schools. *Asia Pacific Journal of Education, 20*(2), 34–45.

Rizvi, F. (2008). Epistemic virtues and cosmopolitan learning: Radford lecture, Adelaide, Australia 27 November 2006. *Australian Educational Researcher, 35*(1), 17–35.

Rizvi, F. (2012). Engaging the Asian century. ACCESS: Critical perspectives on communication. *Cultural & Policy Studies, 31*(1), 73–79.

Rizvi, F., & Lingard, B. (2010). *Globalizing education policy*. Routledge.

Robinson, V. M. J., Lloyd, C. A., & Rowe, K. J. (2008). The impact of leadership on student outcomes: An analysis of the differential effects of leadership types. *Educational Administration Quarterly, 44*(5), 635–674.

Rosch, D. M., & Villanueva, J. C. (2016). Motivation to develop as a leader. *New Directions for Student Leadership, 149*(2016), 49–59.

Schleicher, A., & Organisation for Economic Co-operation Development. (2012). *Preparing teachers and developing school leaders for the 21st century lessons from around the world*. OECD Publishing.

Shay, M., & Lampert, J. (2022). Community according to whom? An analysis of how indigenous 'community' is defined in Australia's *through growth to achievement* report on equity in education. *Critical Studies in Education, 63*(1), 47–63.

Shay, M., Miller, J., & Hameed, S. (2021, August). Exploring excellence in indigenous education in Queensland secondary schools. In *Research conference 2021*. ACER.

Shields, C. M. (2018). *Transformative leadership in education: Equitable change in an uncertain and complex world.* Routledge.

Snook, I., O'Neill, J., Clark, J., O'Neill, A.-M., & Openshaw, R. (2009). Invisible learnings? A commentary on John Hattie's book: Visible learning: A synthesis of over 800 meta-analyses relating to achievement. *New Zealand Journal of Educational Studies, Heidelberg, 44*(1), 93–106.

Stobie, T. (2016). The curriculum battleground. In M. Hayden & J. Thompson (Eds.), *International schools: Current issues and future prospects, symposium books*. Oxford.

Villegas, A. M., & Lucas, T. (2002). Preparing culturally responsive teachers: Rethinking the curriculum. *Journal of Teacher Education, 53*(1), 20–32.

Vongalis-Macrow, A. (2009). The simplicity of educational reforms: Defining globalization and reframing educational policies during the 1990s. *International Journal of Educational Policies, 3*(2), 62–80.

Weinstein, C. S., Tomlinson-Clarke, S., & Curran, M. (2004). Toward a conception of culturally responsive classroom management. *Journal of Teacher Education, 55*(1), 25–38.

Wenner, J. A., & Campbell, T. (2017). The Theoretical and Empirical Basis of Teacher Leadership: A Review of the Literature. *Review of Educational Research, 87*(1), 134–171. https://doi.org/10.3102/0034654316653478

Wilkinson, J., Niesche, R., & Eacott, S. (Eds.). (2018). *Challenges for public education: Reconceptualising educational leadership, policy and social justice as resources of hope*. Routledge.

Wu, H., & Shen, J. (2022). The association between principal leadership and student achievement: A multivariate meta-meta-analysis. *Educational Research Review, 35*. https://doi.org/10.1016/j.edurev.2021.100423

Zeller, D. (2015). *A new theory of leadership: Cosmopolitan leadership – a model for virtual corporations*. www.academia.edu/12166018/Cosmopolitan_Leadership

5   Infrastructures for education
Equity, community, and place

5.0   Introduction

This chapter explores the role played by infrastructure investment in preparing schools for rapidly changing 21st century contexts. We highlight challenges and opportunities associated with infrastructure investment in various educational jurisdictions. To accomplish this, we first explore the issue of residualisation, both in terms of concentrations of disadvantage in particular schools as well as thinking about assets that such schools produce. We then consider the importance of long-term planning to support stability and achieve strategic objectives, including responding to and anticipating demographic shifts. We note the imperative to prepare for technologically rich futures while addressing the associated challenges of digital inequity over time and across contexts and the ongoing challenge of achieving equitable education across location and context.

5.1   Residualisation

A range of policies and practices have contributed to the emergence of residualised schools (Rowe & Perry, 2022). Over the past four decades, education scholars have extensively critiqued neoliberal policy that has cultivated market-based reforms, driven privatisation of education (contributing to residualisation in public education), and entrenched inequitable educational and social outcomes (Gavin et al., 2022). As with most complex contemporary issues, there are few easy answers to how these factors can be mitigated or redirected, but contemporary research does suggest emerging directions and insights.

5.1.1   Insights from comparative school segregation research

Recent comparative research on the causes and effects of school segregation reveals that jurisdictions across the globe are grappling with the challenges of marketisation, school autonomy, and choice. While this comparative research recognizes that overcoming residualisation is challenging, insights into the causes of segregation offer ways forward. Perry et al. (2022) argue that there are three

DOI: 10.4324/9781032666839-5

overlapping domains that are important in considering the reasons for segregation: (1) psycho-social factors, (2) contextual and societal factors, and (3) educational ecosystems, which include a wide range of settings, structures, processes, and policy settings.

The psycho-social domain 'captures the social "laws" that relate to the relationship between schooling and society and that influence and explain how households choose schooling for their children and youths in their care' (p. 4). There are five dynamics at play in this domain that explain how and why households choose schools, which are associated with status and social positioning:

> (1) education is a main vehicle for social reproduction and mobility in modern societies; (2) parents want, at the minimum, to maintain their social status and position; (3) the higher one's social status, the more one 'needs' education to reproduce one's status; (4) therefore, higher status families are more likely to engage in school choice than other families; (5) large differences between schools increase the 'need,' perceived or actual, to engage in choice.
>
> (Adapted from p. 4)

Reflecting the influence of contextual and societal factors (second domain), these five dynamics raise questions about social inequality that are also connected to social class, gender, ethnicity and race, population and immigration dynamics, degrees of income inequality and the 'nature and degree of residential and other forms of spatial segregation' (p. 5).

The third domain in Perry et al.'s (2022) theoretical framework about the causes of school segregation – educational ecosystems – is perhaps the most important for our purposes, and particularly how they intersect with the other two domains. More research is required to illuminate these relationships and suggest ways forward that address the key, complex drivers of residualisation within educational ecosystems. However, alongside more detailed insights into such ecosystems, some possible solutions are emerging, which we also outline in more detail here.

Chesters and Cuervo (2022) found that students attending non-urban/suburban (regional and rural) schools are disadvantaged by fewer curriculum offerings and lower quality resources and infrastructure, which are also more challenging for these students to access. As Dean et al. (2023) found, 'even after controlling for family background and achievement, there is a strong relationship between subject availability in the final year of school, and post-school study and career choices' (p. 1). Their research drew on a large sample of 73, 351 students across 770 schools in New South Wales.

These authors also noted that opportunities to access the academic curriculum are closely associated with school socioeconomic composition. For example, schools in the three highest socio-economic (ICSEA) quartiles offer a greater range of academic subjects and more advanced subjects than schools in the lowest quartile. Schools in the lowest quartile tend to offer fewer advanced subjects in the core areas of English and mathematics and more vocational subjects. There is also a strong correlation between school socio-educational advantage, the number and complexity of subjects offered, and overall student achievement in results in the Higher School Certificate in this state (at the end of the final year of schooling). Further, Dean et al. (2023) also suggest that enrolment size, school sector, and the single-sex affiliation of schools also affect access to the academic curriculum at the most advanced levels. For example, enrolment size is impacted by social composition and marketisation. This aligns with previous research showing that schools with more disadvantaged students have less diverse curriculum offerings. Sector differences also exist between government schools and independent schools, as well as within government schools. Highly resourced private schools and selective government schools (in which low SES students are underrepresented) offer more curriculum choice than government schools and lower fee private and/or religiously affiliated schools.

To address these inequities, a politics of distribution is recommended to allow regional and rural and low SES students' educational opportunities to align with their aspirations. Further, a 'politics of recognition' associated with recognising and valuing rural regions and local communities would help overcome the lower status associated with education in particular areas. To realise these distribution and recognition goals, a range of possible policy directions are suggested.

For example, easing the burden of financial and non-financial costs of relocation away from family and community support, which are not covered by sufficient welfare payments, would better support regional and rural students to access education services in metropolitan areas. Often, young people from low socioeconomic backgrounds are blamed for a lack of educational aspirations. However, as Corbett and Forsey (2017) note, these young people have similar aspirations to their urban peers but often do not have the same economic or geographical resources to enact them. As such, remediating economic and geographical constraints is a practical strategy for helping marginalised young people to realise their ambitions. Alternatively (or additionally), increasing and improving local study options would mean that students don't necessarily need to move away from their support networks to access education.

Another strategy is to provide incentives to encourage young people to return to rural and regional areas, and less advantaged areas, upon completing their education. Research indicates that most students who leave rural and regional areas for further study do not return after completing higher education, which means these areas lose their most talented and capable young people. These structural inequalities are exacerbated by policies of marketisation and school choice, which 'drive schools towards offering distinct curriculum pathways to either remain competitive in attracting students or opting out of such competition and serving the residual needs of marginalised communities increasingly segregated by social background' (p. 16). In these circumstances, attracting accomplished professionals, including teachers, to regional, rural and lower SES areas is essential; this can improve and enrich community life more broadly, generating richer local study and employment options that can challenge structural inequalities.

To address such inequities, and drawing upon the Australian context, Bonnor et al. (2021) document and challenge 'structural failure' in education. Their suggestions include making choice fairer, embedding equity and monitoring and acting on the results of equity-oriented activity in schools. They argue for keeping a strong state to support schooling systems while also making a case for education as a public good. Most crucially, they argue for investing and trusting in teachers and ensuring that the teaching profession is at the heart of attempts at structural reform. (See *Appendix F* for further elaboration of these points.)

5.1.2   Insights from Independent Public Schools (IPS)

There are also lessons to be learnt from the Australian context about supporting schools from the Independent Public School (IPS) initiative, which devolves greater responsibility to individual schools and is an important policy driver in relation to residualisation. Western Australia is regarded as a leader in this model, which has also been taken up in other states and territories and in jurisdictions overseas (e.g. charter schools in the United States). Western Australia's diverse population is spread unevenly across a vast territory. This has led to a focus on decentralising and devolving responsibility to individual schools in an effort, putatively, to be more responsive to local community needs (Fitzgerald et al., 2018; Forsey, 2009). At different times, federal governments have also contended that IPSs increase school choice and control and strengthen 'links between schools, parents and the local community' (Australian Government, 2016 in Kimber, 2020, p. 532).

Scholarship indicates, however, that the IPS model encourages competition among schools, including in already disadvantaged areas. As such, IPS models 'benefit some struggling schools . . . but . . . at the expense of other schools' (Fitzgerald et al., 2018, p. 675). Similarly, Keddie et al. (2020) note that despite continuing strong public and policy support for achieving more autonomous schools, there is evidence that rather than improving academic outcomes, devolving responsibility to schools 'continues to exacerbate inequity within and between schools and their systems' (p. 432). Rowe and Perry (2022) also found that selective schools are dominated by students from more privileged backgrounds and that school choice/autonomy and competition contribute to residualisation of public schools more broadly. (This situation is further exacerbated by the publication of standardised test results, ostensibly for accountability and transparency purposes, but which have contributed to increased competition and residualisation of schools in some jurisdictions [Kimber, 2020].)

This does not mean that principals should not be more autonomous in their decision-making. Keddie et al. (2020) foreground the importance of principals being supported to realise the potential benefits of school autonomy 'in ways that adequately support all students' (p. 442). School leaders need to enact their autonomy in ways that are not only about performativity, compliance, competition, and regulation, but which take into account a range of student interests and in ways that challenge restrictions on enrolment, leading to elitism (Keddie et al., 2018). Keddie et al. (2020) point to recent work by Heffernan and Pierpoint (2020), which offers a range of recommendations in relation to policy, practices and structures that can support principals to realise school autonomy in ways that also take account of issues of student equity. Key recommendations include the following:

- Clarifying and better defining the role of contemporary principals, leaders and education authorities
- Deploying targeted policies and programs to attract and retain principals, including a focus on wellbeing
- Providing professional learning support for principals that addresses key issues around autonomy
- Revising supervision structures to support a model of 'walking beside' principals

5.1.3   Insights from green infrastructure and disaster scholarship

There is also evidence to suggest that overcoming residualisation in schools is linked to community involvement and ownership, but the key question here is how to bring such involvement and ownership about. Research on green infrastructure projects with/in schools offers one possible approach.

With regard to concentrations of disadvantage, Chawla (2018) argues that disadvantaged students and families particularly benefit from access to nature at schools; indeed, 'nature-based learning can help close the achievement gap' (p. xxvii) by enhancing student wellbeing, attention, and academic outcomes (see also Hughes et al. (2019) and Largo-Wight et al. (2018)). Ideally, local green infrastructure projects should be initiated by community members. As such, schools need to engage with local community stakeholders from conception and sustain participatory approaches throughout the planning process (Lovell & Taylor, 2013). Wilson (2018) offers further valuable insights into how to genuinely engage vulnerable and disadvantaged communities in infrastructure projects. Likewise, research undertaken through projects such as the *Logan Together* initiative in south-east Queensland offers an example of working with the community to generate ideas for how to create meaningful connections between community members and education. The approach taken is one guided by both collective impact (government agencies, researchers, schools working together) and drawing upon children's voices as part of consultation processes (see Logan Together, 2021); this work is underpinned by childist principles (Wall, 2022).

Additionally, green infrastructure projects can be leveraged during disaster recovery and planning – arguably an increasingly frequent event (see Tashiro, 2021). Globally, disasters, such as drought, fire, and floods, are becoming more common and more expensive (Crosweller & Tschakert, 2021; Finucane et al., 2020). Being responsive to this challenge is particularly salient in schools, which play an important role in social cohesion and in supporting recovery and enhancing resilience during disasters. Scholarship in this area is, however, relatively scant. In their literature review of strategies to promote educational access during crises, Burde et al. (2015) noted that there is a dearth of research that investigates how to promote educational access in disaster-affected countries and regions. However, the negative effects of destruction or disruption of infrastructure as a result of natural disasters has been clearly shown to have negative effects on school-aged children (Caruso, 2017).

The disruption caused by the COVID-19 pandemic is another challenge to which schools have had to respond. While the legacy of these disruptions for personal and working life continues to unfold, government and non-government bodies and systems must nevertheless plan for and respond to this shifting landscape. This has implications for school enrolment patterns, residualisation, and the built environment in schools. In Queensland, Australia, enrolment in distance education is 12% higher than before the pandemic (O'Flaherty, 2021), and it was recently reported that 'one education Minister has called for permanent changes to the school system after some students performed better during remote learning' (Sacks et al., 2020). Interestingly, private school enrolments have increased during the pandemic, increasing six times faster than state school enrolments (Bita, 2022). However, it is also important to note that such trends were occurring prior to 2020; Independent Schools Queensland [ISQ] reported that enrolments increased by 4.5% between August 2019 and 2020 (Independent Schools Queensland, 2021). Such findings are in keeping with associated research indicating private school drift is ongoing and constitutes a form of 'meta-privatisation' which also potentially overshadows marketisation processes and resourcing gaps between public secondary schools (Rowe, 2020).

When recovering from disaster, activities that would normally take place over time are instead compressed ('time compression'), e.g. repairing schools damaged by flood. This can contribute to difficulties associated with coping with such disasters (Finucane et al., 2020). Making decisions with long-term implications early – while disaster recovery is already underway – can reduce the effectiveness of vulnerability mitigation in the longer term. This highlights both the importance of long-term infrastructure planning to reduce the impact of disasters as well as the challenges of making decisions with long-term implications during the immediate recovery period. Employing appropriate theoretical frameworks, such as the *Sendai Framework for Disaster Risk Reduction* can assist with long-term infrastructure planning for disaster. This framework encourages recovery that restores and rebuilds to mitigate future vulnerabilities, i.e. 'build back better.'

To this end, valuable opportunities also exist to build on Indigenous knowledges around environmental management practices. Marshall (2020) argues that Indigenous knowledge systems are critical to sustainable change. Given that Traditional Knowledge Systems (TKS) have already been employed in a range of domains, including architecture, construction, planning, and urban design, it stands to reason that TKS can and should be integrated into green infrastructure projects in schools. The connection of such infrastructure design to Indigenous curricula more broadly (such as the Aboriginal and Torres Strait Islander Histories and Cultures Cross-curriculum priority in the Australian context) is also important.

Key message: National and international policies have cultivated a climate of school marketisation and competition, which has had deleterious effects on schools, students, school leaders, and other stakeholders. Exacerbating these challenges are factors such as natural disasters, which are potentially increasing in frequency and effect.

Ways forward: To reduce residualisation and address associated trends and challenges, policies around school choice need to be refined to maximise benefits to students in schools while minimising disadvantages. Strategies include supporting principals and school leaders to enact choice in ways that take into consideration the overlapping domains that cause segregation while planning for and building stronger connections with community.

5.2 The impact on schools of 'clustered,' 'precinct,' or broader place-based approaches

In this section, we highlight research around the affordances of technological and digital infrastructures and how place-based stakeholder infrastructure building approaches can help solve 'problems that matter' (Brennan et al., 2020) in education. Various examples of research that relate to place-based approaches are also provided. A key message is that overcoming residualisation in a marketised, competitive schooling system requires taking a long view that focuses on equity through forming long-term school-community connections and capacity building.

5.2.1 Clustering and technological/digital infrastructures

Globally, schools have sought to create digitally rich learning environments for students to prepare them for technologically ubiquitous 21st-century life and work. However, despite these efforts, inequities – also known as the digital divide – remain because of complex ecologies in and around schools. These complex ecologies include school funding, teachers' educational practices, the ways schools seek to mitigate digital inequity, and students' socioeconomic and cultural backgrounds (Kim et al., 2021). Further, it is often wrongly assumed that young people are 'digital natives' who know how to use technology. This notion of the 'digital native' has been highly critiqued as a myth that can disadvantage students when assumptions about competence are made (Drane et al., 2021).

Geographical circumstance is another key element which influences access to adequate technological/digital infrastructures. In many countries, technologies supplied to rural communities are often inferior to those in more metropolitan and suburban communities. Freeman et al. (2020) argue that 'the form and quality of access still shape the activities undertaken online, and inequities often remain due to forced reliance upon expensive, unreliable, poor-quality broadband outside urban areas' (p. 1949). This contributes to digital inequity experienced by people living and working in rural settings (Freeman et al., 2020) including school communities. Furthermore, Drane et al. (2021) contend that the pandemic exacerbated existing educational disadvantage amongst students who already lacked access to computers and/or reliable internet. In short, technological infrastructure and resources are critical to meaningful use of technology in education (Bozkuş, 2021), but complex and interwoven barriers remain.

In recent years, there has been a shift in scholarly thinking away from a binary notion of digital access/lack of access to a more nuanced understanding of digital inclusion and digital exclusion. Contemporary thinking conceives the digital divide not only as the gap between those with access to new technologies and those without (due to factors such as socioeconomic status, gender, race, and ethnicity (van Dijk, 2020)), but also 'considers the availability of ICT infrastructure and the ability, confidence, and experience to effectively use digital technology' (Bennett et al., 2020). As such, it is insufficient to think of digital/technological infrastructure alone as the key to bridging this divide – we must also consider more human and less easily quantifiable dimensions, such as ability, confidence, and other digital dispositions (McLay et al., 2023). Building networks among schools and between schools and their communities is crucial (Bigum, 2004). This approach puts the building of community at the centre of technology use. Knowledge-producing schools, where schools become sources of knowledge for and about their communities, are one example of such an approach (see Bigum & Rowan, 2009).

5.2.2   Reframing infrastructure planning through place-based, bottom-up approaches

A thorough review of primary schools as community hubs (Sanjeevan et al., 2012) shows that while a variety of approaches to the use of these schools to energise communities exist internationally, such hubs are dependent on the following:

- Consultation: resources for consulting with diverse stakeholders around community needs
- Leadership: support to create passionate, committed leadership that can generate support across multiple levels (e.g. principals, departments)
- Evaluation: tools and strategies for evaluating school-community hubs
- Funding: how to locate and leverage funding opportunities
- Engaging vulnerable families and family involvement: locally effective approaches supported by case studies
- Family-friendly service environments: identifying their features and strategies for establishment
- Building community capacity: locally effective approaches and strategies (pp. 42–43)

With regard to consultation and community capacity building, the research conducted by Lingard et al. (2014), as reported in the PETRA project (Pursuing Equity Through Rich Accountabilities), exemplifies the importance of some of these factors. PETRA was conducted in regional Queensland, Australia, with eight schools (five secondary schools and three primary schools). The project was carried out in collaboration with the Queensland Department of Education and Training (DET). The overarching goal of the project was to contribute to the construction of a richer conception of educational accountability than current, test-based modes that have become prevalent not only in Australia but around the world. As part of this work, it was noted that principals indicated and were concerned about the disjuncture between political pressure to ensure enhanced short-term outcomes in relation to funding provision, and how any substantive educational reform necessarily takes a much longer time to develop, cultivate and bring into being (Lingard et al., 2014). The PETRA project sought to develop 'rich accountabilities' (between all participants involved – students, teachers, parents, broader community) while pursuing equity. Such an approach is germane to thinking about residualisation and meaningful community engagement in infrastructure development.

Part of this work involved the establishment of a Learning Commission which was based on highly effective research conducted by Sarah Whatmore (Whatmore, 2009; Whatmore & Landström, 2011) in the UK to deal with flood mitigation. Whatmore developed what she named as 'competency groups,' which are 'forums for collaborative thinking' (Whatmore & Landström, 2011, p. 586). These forums are established so that stakeholders affected by the outcomes of possible solutions to problems have a direct say in what these solutions might be. The success of such competency groups relies on working with people who are directly affected, and who can articulate their ideas about possible solutions. In their research, Lingard et al. (2014) noted that the establishment of the competency group was not at all straightforward and suggested that it 'takes time to build trust and engage community members in a process of this kind' (Lingard et al., 2021, p. 584). This approach can be seen as one step towards reinvigorating democracy and extending the role of citizens beyond 'being dependents on professional knowledge' or simply as 'consumers' of schooling (Ranson, 2018, p. 56).

The PETRA project attempted to link schools together and more tightly to their communities. Further work on similar initiatives flags the significance of community hubs as critical infrastructures (McShane & Coffey, 2022). The success of such community hubs is dependent on the following 'moves.' First, there is a need to move from a transactional approach to community infrastructure development to a more participatory one; such an approach favours 'policy attention and resource allocation directed towards preparation and resilience' (p. 3). Second, there is a need to move from a place-focused to a place-based approach; this involves a shift to 'where 'policy is "done with," rather than "done to"'' (p. 4). Third, there is a need to combine and build on the socio-technical and social emotional dimensions of infrastructure for community. Finally, there is a need to conceive of change as both transitional and transformational. In so doing, change is enabled both within existing systems and understandings, as well through challenging long-standing practices and the effects of such practices.

5.2.3   *Forward, future-facing, equity capacity-building through place-based social connection*

Research on partnerships between universities and schools suggests that partnerships between schools, and between clusters of schools and universities, are important. Recent research from Lisbon found that collaborative work within school clusters was dependent on caring and trusting relationships between those involved (Costa et al., 2022). The themes of joint activities, and trust and caring, are important and link with other collaborative work (for example, with communities) in schools serving high-poverty communities (see FitzGerald & Quiñones, 2019).

5.2.4   Social pedagogy to build place-based infrastructure

Broadly, social pedagogy refers to educational measures that address social purposes. Social pedagogy can be seen in specialised interventions in continental Europe, such as elder care, residential childcare, and fostering, as well as in mainstream programmes such as after-school clubs. The term 'social pedagogy' has a long history, referring to work done by theorists and reformers even prior to the field's formal recognition/definition in 1841 (Petrie, 2002). As Hämäläinen (2003) notes, education was placed at the centre of efforts to address pressing social issues: 'From the outset, the social pedagogical viewpoint was centred on attempts to identify educational answers to social issues' (p. 71). Hämäläinen (2012) also observed that social pedagogy has evolved in two directions: first, towards the prevention and reduction of social exclusion and, second, more broadly towards the promotion of welfare, communal life, and the social development of the individual and the larger society. Social pedagogy conceives learning as a process that occurs when the social pedagogue is working 'alongside' people as a supportive, egalitarian presence. The Social Pedagogy Professional Association (SPPA) based in the UK has a wealth of resources that are worth exploring for those interested in learning more about this movement (https://sppa-uk.org/).

Key message: Working with residualised schools and their communities on 'problems that matter' to them offers a long-term way to address the complexity of segregation in the public schooling sector. Strong support for school leadership and staff to commit to this process and build relational trust over time are vital (Mayger & Hochbein, 2021). The PETRA project highlights the possibilities and challenges of a regional approach and the complexities of schools working together on shared problems.

Ways forward: The following strategies assist with building stronger, place-based approaches to learning: (1) employ teachers and school leaders to stay for the long term in one school, (2) invest in building capacity in the school and community for engagement about long term problems in the community, (3) work to overcome the alienation from residualised schools that many people in underserved communities feel by opening schools up to ongoing community access (see Heimans et al., 2021), and (4) provide incentives for schools that serve a local community to work together to share resources and data to enhance learning in all schools (and the wider community).

5.3 Conclusion

In their research on high-performing schools in the USA, Anderson et al. (2020) note that schools have the capacity to either enhance or diminish social equity for different groups that have traditionally been residualised in public education. This is similarly borne out in Australian research where there is evidence that schooling has increasingly undermined social equity through school choice, even as broader policy settings maintain equity as a key goal (Bonnor et al., 2021). This all suggests that problems surrounding broader social infrastructure investment are complex and that the root causes of residualisation are associated with marketisation and competition. There are also other broad factors that impact on residualisation. For example, it is well established that digital disruption and ongoing rapid change exacerbate differences. The impact of climate change, such as increasingly intense and frequent floods, droughts, and fire, now widely acknowledged as a global emergency and requiring immediate, ongoing attention (Crosweller & Tschakert, 2021), will also impact most strongly on those schools and communities with the fewest resources to respond to such conditions.

There is, however, some evidence of potential ways forward. These are to be found in approaches to operating schools that aim to build strong, sustainable, long-term relationships between schools and communities while recognising that schools serve important functions as drivers of change in communities (Masschelein & Simons, 2013). While schools cannot compensate for society, as Bernstein (1970) argued more than half a century ago, we do need to ask what kind of schools society needs and what kind of society schools need (see Biesta, 2019, 2021). Systems can support school leaders and teachers in residualised schools to commit to working over the long term in the school and for the community – working on the real problems that the community faces (for example, intergenerational trauma and long-term poverty) and that schools can actually do something about. There is also clearly a need to rethink how schooling accountability systems operate (with a need for greater attention to 'rich' accountabilities for example). Further, there are lessons from approaches to supporting schools that may not be directly focused on overcoming residualisation but will nonetheless achieve some benefits in this regard; a social pedagogy approach, for example, may assist some schools in such work. Various green infrastructure projects are also useful for thinking differently about equity-oriented investment that addresses urgent intractable social, economic, and environmental challenges that are simultaneously local and global in nature. Yet we also reiterate that problems that are seemingly solvable by teachers or schools may reflect broader systemic challenges. As such, it is necessary to enact policy that takes into account social and physical infrastructure needs that do not simply take into account the performance of individual students and schools, but also broader systemic performance and socio-economic conditions, so as to provide the necessarily wide array of resources for communities, schools, and students to flourish.

5.4 Chapter questions

1. In your context, has there been a rise in or diminution of trust and investment in teachers? What has been the main cause of this change, and what can you do about it?

2. Are you aware of the effects of the privatisation and marketisation of public schooling in your nation state? How have or might these effects be ameliorated?
3. Are there education policies in your context that take seriously the interrelations between climate change, infrastructure investment, and education? How successful are these policies and what further changes could be beneficial in this regard?
4. How can schools become positive agents of change for their students and the communities that they serve? What are the examples of this, for example, in situations of high poverty, in your context?
5. In your context, how possible is it for performativity to be resisted? What are some ways of working together as educators to foster an educational sense of what matters in schools, against the current policy landscape that valorises data, high-stakes assessment outcomes, and achievement for its own sake?
6. How might the school/system you work in become more genuinely knowledge-producing?
7. How might an engagement with social pedagogy enhance the democratic potential of your school/system and/or work to foster stronger relations among students, staff, and community?

5.5 References

Anderson, T., Blom, E., Lindsay, C., Rosenboom, V., Gebrekristos, S., Rainer, M., & Vilter, C. (2020). *Identifying high-performing schools for historically underserved students: Exploring a multistate model*. Urban Institute.

Australian Government. (2016). *Quality schools, quality outcomes*. https://docs.education.gov.au/documents/quality-schools-quality-outcomes

Bennett, R., Uink, B., & Cross, S. (2020). Beyond the social: Cumulative implications of COVID-19 for first nations university students in Australia. *Social Sciences & Humanities Open, 2*(1). https://doi.org/10.1016/j.ssaho.2020.100083

Bernstein, B. (1970). Education cannot compensate for society. *New Society, 26*, 344–345.

Biesta, G. (2019). What kind of society does the school need? Redefining the democratic work of education in impatient times. *Studies in Philosophy and Education, 38*, 657–668.

Biesta, G. (2021). *World-centred education: A view for the present*. Routledge.

Bigum, C. (2004). Rethinking schools and community: The knowledge producing schools. In S. Marshall, W. Taylor, & X. Yu (Eds.), *Using community informatics to transform regions* (pp. 52–66). IGI Global.

Bigum, C., & Rowan, L. (2009). Renegotiating knowledge relationships in schools. In S. E. Noffke & B. Somekh (Eds.), *The SAGE handbook of educational action research* (pp. 102–109). Sage.

Bita, N. (2022, February 23). Private schools poach students with hi-tech teaching. *The Australian*.

Bonnor, C., Kidson, P., Piccoli, A., Sahlberg, P., & Wilson, R. (2021). *Structural failure: Why Australia keeps falling short of its educational goals*. UNSW Gonski Institute.

Bozkuş, K. (2021). Digital devices and student achievement: The relationship in PISA 2018 data. *International Online Journal of Education and Teaching, 8*(3), 1560–1579.

Brennan, M., Taylor, S., & Zipin, L. (2020). Students researching 'problems that matter' in their communities. *Forum, 62*(2), 195–206.

Burde, D., Guven, O., Kelcey, J., Lahmann, H., & Al-Abbadi, K. (2015). What works to promote children's educational access, quality of learning, and wellbeing in crisis-affected contexts. In *Education rigorous literature review, department for international develop-ment*. Department for International Development.

Caruso, G. D. (2017). The legacy of natural disasters: The intergenerational impact of 100 years of disasters in Latin America. *Journal of Development Economics, 127*, 209–233.

Chawla, L. (2018). Nature-based learning for student achievement and ecological citizen-ship. *Curriculum and Teaching Dialogue, 20*(1), xxv–xxxix.

Chesters, J., & Cuervo, H. (2022). (In) equality of opportunity: Educational attainments of young people from rural, regional and urban Australia. *The Australian Educational Researcher, 49*(1), 43–61.

Corbett, M., & Forsey, M. (2017). Rural youth out-migration and education: Challenges to aspirations discourse in mobile modernity. *Discourse: Studies in the Cultural Politics of Education, 38*(3), 429–444.

Costa, E., Baptista, M., & Dorotea, N. (2022). Supporting schools in times of crisis: A case of partnerships and networking with schools by the institute of education at the university of Lisbon. In *University and school collaborations during a pandemic* (pp. 211–224). Springer.

Crosweller, & Tschakert, P. (2021). Disaster management and the need for a reinstated social contract of shared responsibility. *International Journal of Disaster Risk Reduction, 63*. https://doi.org/10.1016/j.ijdrr.2021.102440

Dean, J., Roberts, P., & Perry, L. B. (2023). School equity, marketisation and access to the Australian senior secondary curriculum. *Educational Review, 75*(2), 243–263.

Drane, C. F., Vernon, L., & O'Shea, S. (2021). Vulnerable learners in the age of COVID-19: A scoping review. *The Australian Educational Researcher, 48*, 585–604.

Finucane, M., Acosta, J., Wicker, A., & Whipkey, K. (2020). Short-term solutions to a long-term challenge: Rethinking disaster recovery planning to reduce vulnerabilities and inequities. *International Journal of Environmental Research and Public Health, 17*(2), 482. https://doi.org/10.3390/ijerph17020482

FitzGerald, A. M., & Quiñones, S. (2019). Working in and with community: Leading for partnerships in a community school. *Leadership and Policy in Schools, 18*(4), 511–532.

Fitzgerald, S., Stacey, M., McGrath-Champ, S., Parding, K., & Rainnie, A. (2018). Devolu-tion, market dynamics and the independent public school initiative in Western Australia: 'Winning back' what has been lost? *Journal of Education Policy, 33*(5), 662–681.

Forsey, M. (2009). The problem with autonomy: An ethnographic study of neoliberalism in practice at an Australian high school. *Discourse: Studies in the Cultural Politics of Education, 30*(4), 457–469.

Freeman, J., Park, S., & Middleton, C. (2020). Technological literacy and interrupted inter-net access. *Information, Communication & Society, 23*(13), 1947–1964.

Gavin, M., McGrath-Champ, S., Wilson, R., Fitzgerald, S., & Stacey, M. (2022). Teacher workload in Australia: National reports of intensification and its threats. In S. Riddle, A. Heffernan, & D. Bright (Eds.), *New perspectives on education for democracy: Creative responses to local and global challenges* (pp. 110–123). Routledge.

Hämäläinen, J. (2003). The concept of social pedagogy in the field of social work. *Journal of Social Work, 3*(1), 69–80.

Hämäläinen, J. (2012). Social pedagogical eyes in the midst of diverse understandings, con-ceptualisations and activities. *International Journal of Social Pedagogy, 1*(1), 3–16.

Heffernan, A., & Pierpoint, A. (2020). *Autonomy, accountability, and principals' work: An Australian study*. Australian Secondary Principals' Association.

Heimans, S., Singh, P., & Barnes, A. (2021). Researching educational disadvantage: Con-cepts emerging from working in/with an Australian school. *Improving Schools, 24*(2), 182–192.

Hughes, H., Franz, J., & Willis, J. (Eds.). (2019). *School spaces for student wellbeing and learning: Insights from research and practice*. Springer.

ISQ (Independent Schools Queensland) (2021, February 19). *New data confirms the value of independent schools to Queensland parents* [Media Release]. https://www.isq.qld.edu.au/publications-resources/posts/new-data-confirms-the-value-of-independent-schools-to-queensland-parents/

Keddie, A., Gobby, B., & Wilkins, C. (2018). School autonomy reform in Queensland: Governance, freedom and the entrepreneurial leader. *School Leadership & Management, 38*(4), 378–394.

Keddie, A., MacDonald, C., Blackmore, J., Eacott, S., Gobby, B., Mahoney, C., & Wilkinson, J. (2020). School autonomy, marketisation and social justice: The plight of principals and schools. *Journal of Educational Administration and History, 52*(4), 432–447.

Kim, H. J., Yi, P., & Hong, J. I. (2021). Are schools digitally inclusive for all? Profiles of school digital inclusion using PISA 2018. *Computers and Education, 170*. https://doi.org/10.1016/j.compedu.2021.104226

Kimber, M. (2020). A social justice challenge for school leadership in Australia. In R. Papa (Ed.), *Handbook on promoting social justice in education* (pp. 523–543). Springer.

Largo-Wight, E., Guardino, C., Wludyka, P. S., Hall, K. W., Wight, J. T., & Merten, J. W. (2018). Nature contact at school: The impact of an outdoor classroom on children's well-being. *International Journal of Environmental Health Research, 28*(6), 653–666.

Lingard, B., Baroutsis, A., & Sellar, S. (2021). Enriching educational accountabilities through collaborative public conversations: Conceptual and methodological insights from the learning commission approach. *Journal of Educational Change, 22*(4), 565–587.

Lingard, B., Baroutsis, A., Seller, S., Brennan, M., Mills, M., Renshaw, P., Waters, R., & Zipin, L. (2014). *Learning commission report: Connecting schools with communities.* Queensland Department of Education, Training and Employment.

Logan Together. (2021). *Logan Together.* www.logantogether.org.au/

Lovell, S. T., & Taylor, J. R. (2013). Supplying urban ecosystem services through multifunctional green infrastructure in the United States. *Landscape Ecology, 28*(8), 1447–1463.

Marshall, C. A. (2020). The role of indigenous paradigms and traditional knowledge systems in modern humanity's sustainability quest – future foundations from past knowledges. In R. Roggema (Ed.), *Designing sustainable cities: Contemporary urban design thinking.* Springer.

Masschelein, J., & Simons, M. (2013). *In defence of the school. A public issue.* TStorme.

Mayger, L. K., & Hochbein, C. D. (2021). Growing connected: Relational trust and social capital in community schools. *Journal of Education for Students Placed at Risk (JESPAR), 26*(3), 210–235.

McLay, K. F., Thomasse, L., & Reyes, V. C. (2023). Embracing discomfort in active learning and technology-rich higher education settings: Sensemaking through reflexive inquiry. *Educational Technology Research and Development, 71*, 1161–1177.

McShane, I., & Coffey, B. (2022). Rethinking community hubs: Community facilities as critical infrastructure. *Current Opinion in Environmental Sustainability, 54*. https://doi.org/10.1016/j.cosust.2022.101149

O'Flaherty, A. (2021). *COVID-19 pandemic drives surge in enrolments at independent Queensland schools.* www.abc.net.au/news/2021-08-30/pandemic-drives-surge-in-enrolments-at-qld-independent-schools/100413048

Perry, L. B., Rowe, E., & Lubienski, C. (2022). School segregation: Theoretical insights and future directions, *Comparative Education, 58*(1), 1–15.

Petrie, P. (2002). Social pedagogy: An historical account of care and education as social control. In J. Brannen & P. Moss (Eds.), *Rethinking children's care.* Open University Press.

Ranson, S. (2018). *Education, democratic participation: The making of learning communities.* Routledge.

Rowe, E. (2020). Counting national school enrolment shares in Australia: The political arithmetic of declining public school enrolment. *The Australian Educational Researcher, 47*(4), 517–535.

Rowe, E., & Perry, L. (2022). Voluntary school fees in segregated public schools: How selective public schools turbo-charge inequity and funding gaps, *Comparative Education, 58*(1), 106–123.

Sacks, D., Bayles, K., Taggart, A., & Noble, S. (2020). *COVID-19 and education: How Australian schools are responding and what happens next. Government matters.* Price Waterhouse Coopers (PWC Australia). www.pwc.com.au/government/government-matters/covid-19-education-how-australian-schools-are-responding.html

Sanjeevan, S., McDonald, M., & Moore, T. (2012). *Primary schools as community hubs: A review of the literature.* The Royal Children's Hospital Centre for Community Child Health and the Murdoch Children's Research Institute.

Tashiro, A. (2021). Green self-efficacy for blue-green infrastructure management in a post-disaster recovery phase: Empirical research in a small rural community. *Coastal Engineering Journal, 63*(3), 408–421.

van Dijk, J. A. G. M. (2020). *The digital divide.* Polity.

Wall, J. (2022). From childhood studies to childism: Reconstructing the scholarly and social imaginations, *Children's Geographies, 20*(3), 257–270.

Whatmore, S. J. (2009). Mapping knowledge controversies: Science, democracy and the redistribution of expertise. *Progress in Human Geography, 33*(5), 587–598.

Whatmore, S. J., & Landström, C. (2011). Flood apprentices: An exercise in making things public. *Economy and society, 40*(4), 582–610.

Wilson, B. (2018). *Resilience for all.* Island Press.

6 Conclusion
Shaping school success

6.0 Introduction

We conclude the book by briefly recapping the key insights from each chapter. We then elaborate what we describe as key cross-theme foci that we believe can be usefully derived from a synthesis across each of the chapters. These foci, we argue, are essential for promoting the sorts of individual and collective holistic learning that is necessary for fostering enhanced educational provision in both individual schools and school systems.

6.1 Summary

By elaborating notions of **school performance**, the book began with an overview of system-wide strategies designed to improve educational performance, including various approaches to support educators with identified needs. This chapter was necessarily wide-ranging, given its efforts to understand the plethora of issues that impact school performance overall. However, it also sought to understand such systems as functioning, holistic ecologies that needed to take not just academic performance and school data into account but students' social and emotional health and wellbeing. At the same time, various technologies, such as AI and mobile phones, are increasingly part of the landscape of schooling and need to be engaged much more proactively – as learning resources – than has perhaps been the case in the past.

Holistic education design also entails developing more long-standing understandings of sustainability within schools and school systems and amongst students. This should be an agentic-inducing exercise, in which students can see how research and inquiry can help not only better understand what may seem to be entrenched and 'wicked' problems (e.g. climate change, AI in warfare, educational inequities) but also how to address these. This also involves a much more systematic focus on issues of equity (and inequality) in education and how to address sedimented disadvantage.

Through sharing insights into the nature of **teaching expertise** in all its complexity, the book also sought to elaborate impactful teaching and classroom

DOI: 10.4324/9781032666839-6

management practices which help in this process of addressing disadvantage. Through attention to pedagogical practices that contribute to student learning, as well as the professional development and capability development needed to generate such productive teacher expertise across the teaching career, educational systems can foster genuinely responsive approaches and foci.

Teacher expertise also needs to be oriented towards addressing the needs of students with multiple abilities/disability and diverse learning needs. Indigenous students' needs must be made much more explicit, and broader pedagogical understandings developed and practised must recognise that so many approaches that are responsive to Indigenous and differently abled students are also beneficial for *all* students. Community, collaboration, and being culturally responsive are all key to success.

Developing teacher expertise also involves advocacy for coaching models that are much more likely than traditional PD to foster teacher growth and understanding and, most importantly, change practice in the classroom. Learning communities are only of value if they can be sustained. The specific needs of teachers who are teaching out-of-field also need to be taken into account, as well as those working in rural and remote communities but who do not have the background or expertise to effectively engage their students in these settings.

In terms of in-school factors, issues of **educational leadership** are recognised as second only to teaching practice as major contributors to student learning. While various meta-studies are useful for providing broad insights and overviews of key issues of importance, they are insufficient for cultivating the sorts of context-relevant leadership practice essential to enhancing educational provision in schools today – particularly in the most disadvantaged communities and environments. Issues of inclusivity need to be central to the work of all leaders; equity and social justice are not add-ons but are core to the work of the principalship, and leadership practices more broadly within schools and schooling systems. And in increasingly internationalised contexts, a more globally minded approach is key to success in these culturally diverse, cosmopolitan, and mobile communities and settings.

It is also clearly evident that the administrative burden of the principalship needs to be managed and monitored much more closely than has been the case to date. Overloading school leaders with administrative tasks takes them away from what should be their central role: pedagogical leadership for enhanced student learning in their schools. Principals and other school and system leaders need to feel they have influence and agency over their work, and that they are not simply being done-to in these settings. More flexible accountabilities, which take into account not just the human-elements of leadership practice, but non-human as well, are key.

To maximise these system, teacher and leadership practices, there needs to be clear and unequivocal support for various kinds of **infrastructure investment** to maximise the likelihood of success in these domains. If schools and schooling systems are not to become sites of residualisation – settings where only those who feel they do not have any other choice/option come together – there needs to be a clear and unequivocal advocacy for enhanced provision for the most disenfranchised students and the communities from which they are drawn. Only by focusing sustained attention – and resources – upon these sites and settings, can we ever hope to address the shame that stains so many educational systems around the world – the increased division and discord between educational outcomes (and ultimately life outcomes) of those with the most resources, and those with the least. To fail to do otherwise is to abrogate our responsibilities as educators and as citizens. The sorts of competitive models of schools and schooling that have come to dominate the educational landscape in so many national and sub-national contexts around the world is a legacy of inadequate concern or regard for those who do not have the resources to even begin to 'play this game.'

Only by cultivating more sustainable communities, including via various green infrastructures, can schools and schooling systems begin to rebuild and reinvigorate their central task – student learning for all. Various kinds of clusters, precincts, and knowledge hubs, involving not just schools but schools working in conjunction with other bodies and agencies in their local communities – both public (health, welfare) and private (industry) – will help re-establish the social fabric that has become frayed by decades of more competitive, neoliberal, and managerial practices. Grounded, place-based approaches to learning, incorporating technologically rich approaches and foci, will help redress entrenched traditional and digital divides. By engaging in the development of broader placed-based infrastructures from a more bottom-up perspective, the conditions for educational success will be cultivated.

To this end, we conclude with a number of cross-theme foci that we believe will help bring such an educational environment into being.

6.2   Key cross-theme foci

To help foster reform within and across educational systems and schools, this book has identified five key foci as critical to enhancing educational practice in school jurisdictions – for shaping school success. These pertain to the following:

* *Context as key to building an infrastructure for learning;*
* *A futures-oriented approach to learning in a post-pandemic world;*
* *A career-long emphasis on educators' professional learning needs;*
* *A holistic approach to education provision; and*
* *Equitable access to excellence in educational attainment.*

6.2.1   *Schools in context: An infrastructure for learning*

A key cross-theme focus emerging out of our research is the importance of context. Educational systems need to attend to a range of factors to provide for all students, including those typically/most marginalised in society. Such provision requires adequate and fair funding and resourcing to enable successful individual and collective learning; attention to student and staff wellbeing; the belief that every student has a right to learn and that such learning occurs well prior to formal schooling; the belief that students of all abilities should be catered for in schooling settings, particularly those who may require additional supports to ensure their success; and an understanding that while schools alone cannot solve all social ills, they are an important part of the tapestry of support for enhancing learning opportunities for all members of the community.

These factors need to be expressed in ways that make sense in specific settings and under the particular conditions in which schools and school systems are developed and undertake their work. Schools need to be understood as actively embedded in their communities, and these communities comprise valuable assets that can assist educators working with students in schools. At the same time, schools can serve as critical hubs within communities to bring people together and provide a forum in which varying knowledges, approaches, foci, and perspectives can be appreciated and in which concerns and issues can be addressed.

6.2.2 *Future thinking: Education in a post-pandemic world*

It is important not to become overwhelmed by some of the crisis discourses that sometimes characterise schooling. Instead of focusing so resolutely upon what has not been achieved (e.g. gaps in learning/attainment within and between nation-states/groups), it is important to consider how to actually improve educational practice (Education Council, 2019; Sahlberg, 2022). This includes understanding that it is more beneficial to focus on actual learning rather than giving undue attention to various gaps and losses in learning. It is also more productive to invest in reducing inequalities rather than focusing upon specific aspects of schooling as the source of the 'problem' (e.g. student behaviour, teacher quality, inadequate leadership expertise). It is also more beneficial to take broader ('rich') and deeper ('authentic') approaches to understanding and engaging with issues of accountability, rather than relying upon single-measure indicators, or even multiple measures that may all be of a similar ilk (e.g. more standardised test results). Schools also need to be considered as sites that are inherently educational and responsive to their students' needs – as sites that equip students with the dispositions, understandings and skill-set to be able to engage with complex and as yet unrealised futures. Such future thinking can help enhance educational practice rather than limiting schooling to various deficit discourses.

6.2.3 *A career-long emphasis on professional learning*

A resounding theme throughout our work has been the centrality of learning – not just for students, but for the teachers and system educators who help guide their growth and development. This necessitates ensuring adequate provision for education across *all* stages of educators'/teachers' careers. This includes from pre-service through to a range of in-service professional learning opportunities, and then into supporting school and system administrators in their work of supporting teachers and students in schools. This approach to career development should reflect a spectrum between teachers' initial education (pre-service) through to all stages of their subsequent career (in-service/continuing professional learning), with appropriate attention to building the leadership capacity of educators (at both school and system levels). Such a career-long approach involves developing close(r) relationships between (university-based) teacher education institutions and schools, developing trajectories for second-career teachers that are based on suitable learning strategies that recognise their experiences and capacities (Meijer, 2021), and taking more considered approaches to developing the leadership capacities of aspiring and existing school and system leaders. This is the starting point for the development of a career-long spectrum of learning that should characterise all efforts at system and school-based educational reform.

6.2.4   *A holistic educational approach*

Holistic education balances all the potential dimensions of students' learning, resulting in an overall sense of wellbeing (Inugai-Dixon, 2021). It encompasses ideas that 'all knowledge is interrelated in a curriculum that develops the whole person' (Wright et al., 2016, p. 8). Such an education approach focuses the intellectual, emotional, social, physical, creative/intuitive, aesthetic, and spiritual components of the whole person through egalitarian relationships between students and teachers. A more holistic approach actively values, draws upon, and embeds Indigenous perspectives and protocols/ways of being into the learning experiences of students and teachers. In the Australian context, for example, such a holistic approach to education is consistent with *The Mparntwe (Alice Springs) Education Declaration* (Education Council, 2019), in which education 'plays a vital role in promoting the intellectual, physical, social, emotional, moral, spiritual and aesthetic development and wellbeing of young Australians, and in ensuring the nation's ongoing economic prosperity and social cohesion' (p. 3). Such sentiments are not simply limited to one national context and group(s) of Indigenous peoples but in relation to Indigenous peoples, knowledges, and ways of being and learning around the world.

6.2.5   *Excellence and equity*

So often, notions of excellence and equity are pitted against one another. Within the popular imagery, there is a sense in which efforts to foster equity somehow diminish the quality of the educational experience, while efforts to promote excellence automatically leave many students behind. We contest such simplified binaries, arguing that excellence and equity are intricately intertwined, not mutually exclusive. Alongside Varadharajan et al. (2021), we propose that equity in education is critical for improving quality of life, social mobility and reducing economic burden within communities. At present, education provision is not sufficiently equitable and inclusive and educational gaps for certain demographic groups are widening for children – particularly those students living in low socio-economic and remote or rural areas; living with a disability; having Indigenous, refugee, and asylum-seeking backgrounds; and/or having multiple, intersecting identities.

Furthermore, existing testing measures do not capture holistic learning experiences that occur both inside and outside educational settings, and learning needs to be considered a partnership between schools and the communities in which they are situated.

Such an approach challenges undue attention to standardised testing, one-size-fits-all curriculum, and foregrounds the need to focus more substantively on teaching and staffing issues, bullying and social issues, and ways to ensure not only adequate resource/infrastructure provision but ways to enhance student agency. Rather than engaging in various kinds of risk mitigation and reifying disadvantage, there is a need to openly embrace diversity and difference and to recognise the plurality of approaches and foci that characterise cosmopolitan and multicultural societies as valuable assets for the welfare and sustainability (environmental, social, political, and economic) of such societies more broadly.

6.3 Final remarks

We hope you have found this volume both beneficial and stimulating for your thinking, perhaps encouraging you to think anew about what may have become sedimented practices and processes in schooling settings. In this chapter, and in the book more broadly, we have sought to focus necessary attention upon key domains that require attention if individual schools and the broader systems in which they are located are to achieve genuinely educational ends. In this way, we support a holistic, sustainable approach to education provision in schooling settings that provides the intellectual, cultural, social, and emotional/spiritual resources necessary to empower formal and informal educational leaders to productively and authentically shape school success.

6.4 References

Education Council. (2019). *The Mparntwe (Alice Springs) education declaration.* https://docs.education.gov.au/documents/alice-springs-mparntwe-educationdeclaration

Inugai-Dixon, C. A. (2021). Towards a holistic education: Synergizing a traditional model of transmission with inquiry and SEE Learning. In D. G. Coulson, S. Datta, & M. J. Davies (Eds.), *Educational reform and International Baccalaureate in the Asia-Pacific* (pp. 99–113). IGI Global.

Meijer, P. C. (2021). Quality under pressure in Dutch teacher education. In D. Mayer (Ed.), *Teacher education policy and research: Global perspectives* (pp. 101–111). Springer.

Sahlberg, P. (2022, April 22). *How post-pandemic recovery can help transform Australian schools. Dean's keynote series, 2022: Disrupting and transforming education.* Southern Cross University.

Varadharajan, M., Muir, K., Moore, T., Harris, D., Barker, B., Dakin, P., Lowe, K., Smith, C., Baker, S., & Piccoli, A. (2021). *Amplify insights: Education inequity.* Centre for Social Impact, UNSW Sydney.

Wright, E., Lee, M., Tang, H., & Tsui, G. C. P. (2016). Why offer the International Baccalaureate middle years programme? A comparison between schools in Asia-Pacific and other regions. *Journal of Research in International Education, 15*(1), 3–17.

Appendices

Appendix A

Moving from low-performing to high-performing schools

Typically referred to as turn-around in the US context, Hitt and Meyers (2021) drew upon an initial review of literature into what made school districts more responsive to school, principal, teacher, and student needs.

This work involved:

1. District offices being more responsive to teaching and learning, including having the following:

   a. Greater focus on managing human resources;
   b. Focus on teacher PD more broadly;
   c. Focus on teacher coaching, in particular;
   d. Focus on improving standards-based curriculum, teaching and assessment; and
   e. All undergirded by greater attention to data collected in schools.

2. District offices being more responsive to leading, including having a focus on principal supervision role by both supporting and holding principals accountable.

A broader study by the Center on School Turnaround (Hitt & Meyers, 2021; Meyers et al., 2017) also revealed a number of key practices resulting in a framework for system improvement. Such an approach involved attention to four foci:

1. Systems leadership;
2. Developing and managing talent;
3. Building instructional/teaching infrastructure; and
4. Shifting the culture.

In light of this literature, and empirical research into the practices of schools that were successful in moving from low- to high-performing settings, the following **key practices** were identified to promote systemic improvement from low- to high-performing schools:

1. Turnaround leadership:

   a. Prioritise change for improvement and communicate its urgency (clear policies, structures in place to support stakeholders attain goals).

      i. Through using data, districts and school leaders pinpoint the shortcomings of the school;
      ii. Also, districts and school leaders provide examples of data-backed success within other similar schools that improved;
      iii. District and school leaders devote effort to improving messaging in public-facing materials, like the district and school websites, so that they provide visual, compelling evidence of the leadership's intentions in and confidence about the change initiative;
      iv. Within the school walls, the vision itself is displayed as reminders to students and teachers;
      v. School and district leaders inform staff of non-negotiable changes that will be undertaken but with accompanying assurances of support for teachers.

   b. Monitor both short- and long-term goals (data, milestones for progress, regular feedback on progress, capitalise on momentum):

      i. Provide time for teachers to develop teaching goals;
      ii. Monitor and support (rapid feedback) individual teacher instruction (walk-throughs);
      iii. School (and district) leaders engage in monthly data meetings with teacher teams (each grade; subject level); and
      iv. School and district leaders monitor their own engagement by monitoring teacher and student progress and provide feedback to teachers in faculty meetings.

   c. Customise and target support to address teaching and broader organisational needs (aligning supports with key initiatives and removing other initiatives, responding quickly to needs as they arise):

      i. Develop context-responsive plans;
      ii. Use of both internal data analysis (formative, summative, behaviour, attendance) as well as external standardised tests;
      iii. Reallocate resources as required (e.g. extending contracts, additional ESL staff);
      iv. Redesign school structures, including considering how to embed collaborative time for teachers for shared planning;
      v. District leaders work with school leaders to help prioritise identified needs of particular teachers;
      vi. District and school leaders develop protocols for large, small, and individual teacher meetings;
      vii. District leaders provide both individual support and ensure accountability from and for principals. This includes in relation to goal setting, observations, coaching, and feedback on principal practice.

2. Developing and managing talent:

    a. Recruiting, developing, retaining, and sustaining talent (including succession planning; in-house development programs; programs to retain talent):

        i. Focus on team-based collaborative environment;

        ii. Consideration of incentives (pay; time) for teachers undertaking additional duties to develop other teachers;

        iii. Aligning teacher strengths with organisational aims;

        iv. Provision of leadership opportunities to high-performing teachers;

        v. Recognise and celebrate teachers' efforts formally and informally;

        vi. Clarify key responsibilities/aims to minimise fatigue and overload.

    b. Providing professional learning opportunities (individualised professional learning opportunities; job-embedded coaching; mentoring; use of high-performing coaches, teachers, leaders as models and peer coaches):

        i. Draw upon data to inform teaching practice but also revisit use of data to inform subsequent practice;

        ii. District and school leaders emphasise high-quality teaching and provide refreshers on such teaching;

        iii. Development of effective professional learning communities to examine student work and develop lesson plans to enable enhanced student learning;

        iv. District and school leaders provide opportunities to enable teachers time for peer observation and develop peer mentoring skills;

        v. Develop individual PD plans with teachers' input.

    c. Setting clear performance expectations (explicitly sharing expectations re performance; performance management that includes progress monitoring; capacity to adjust professional learning to attain expectations):

        i. Teachers communicate daily about specific student learning goals to be attained;

        ii. Emphasis on high-quality teaching strategies (rigorous questioning strategies; higher order thinking skills);

        iii. Horizontal and vertical alignment of team structures in schools to enable cohesiveness across grade levels, departments, and schools.

3. Building instructional/teaching infrastructure:

    a. Diagnosing and responding to student learning needs and using those identified needs to drive teaching decisions (includes use of rapid assessment and adjusting teaching and grouping to students' learning needs):

        i. School leaders facilitate development of collaboratively developed formative assessments for use in all grades/subject levels;

        ii. Development of assessment schedule which aligns to district reporting requirements and which involve frequent (weekly) formative assessment;

        iii. Provision of time on a regular basis (fortnightly) for teachers to respond to gaps in student learning identified in formative (and summative) assessment.

b. Providing rigorous evidence-based instruction/teaching (setting high stand-ards and growth expectations for students, provide supports to ensure evidence used for teaching planning, adjust plans as gaps in student learning become apparent):

    i. Provision of time for teachers to develop pacing guides for units of work;

    ii. Development of benchmark/interim assessments within schools that are then calibrated for rigor at district/system level;

    iii. Focus on student learning as evident in data analysis to inform teacher PD.

c. Removing barriers and providing opportunities (including opportunities for students to demonstrate early mastery; partnering with health, wellness, youth organisations to develop competencies for success):

    i. Adjust schedules and professional learning community (PLC) foci to better support students in need;

    ii. Rapidly develop plans to support teachers who may be struggling to enhance student learning and to support cohorts of students where there are patterns of need/evidence of lower learning outcomes;

    iii. Development of district and school early-intervention teams to address needs of struggling students.

4. Shifting the culture:

a. A strong culture focused on student learning (celebrating success, developing mastery learning experiences, providing opportunities for community members to collaborate to explore future possibilities):

    i. Recognise student achievement – both attainment of benchmarks and work towards such benchmarks;

    ii. Foster school-wide positive behaviour programs that help support academic attainment;

    iii. Facilitate students' sense of being known and cared for, e.g. via smaller/dedicated pastoral groups;

    iv. Foster student ownership and setting of academic goals.

b. Soliciting and acting upon stakeholder input (gathering and considering overall perceptions, as well as specific stakeholder group perceptions; acting on constructive feedback):

    i. Partner with health and wellness organisations to address dental, medical, nutritional needs;

    ii. Invite community/local business leaders to school to enhance interactions between school and community;

    iii. Gather teacher feedback via formal (e.g. surveys) and informal (e.g. teacher meetings) means.

c. Engaging students and their families in pursuing educational goals (including building students' resilience and self-directedness, providing opportunities for students to connect their learning to outside school, and engaging families in students' growth and development):

   i. Ensure parents from all backgrounds are involved in parent-teacher associations;

   ii. District and school leaders hold preliminary meetings and use multiple modes of communication to share expectations regarding student attendance and performance;

   iii. Focus on ways to increase parent engagement in schools, including supporting teachers to facilitate parents visiting classrooms throughout the year, including to assist with support for individual students.

(Hitt & Meyers, 2021)

Appendix B

Key elements of professional education

Professional Excellence	Strengthen the clinical component and provide a more connected and school-based form of teacher education. Increase attention to research into teaching as an important competence for teachers.
Ethical Responsibility	Consider teachers' ethical responsibilities in a range of curricula from hidden to implemented curricula. Develop ethical educational programs to empower teachers to foster pluralistic and more complex attitudes towards ethical issues more broadly. Develop teachers' ability to recognise complex ethical issues in school contexts to identify ethical dilemmas in context and develop alternatives and understandings of implications of actions taken.
Innovation	Foster understanding of teachers as learning designers who can draw upon available technologies to innovate their teaching to better facilitate student learning. Such purposeful learning will enable greater understanding of a variety of multimodal technologies, including various online apps and social media.

(Adapted from Tang & Cheng, 2021, pp. 90–93)

Appendix C

Ten key themes to help support quality teaching for every child

1. A high social regard for teaching, expressed in government statements and actions about teaching.
2. Selectivity into the profession, enabled by teaching's high status and strong support.
3. Financial support for preparation and professional learning: With preparation largely or entirely subsidised, all candidates can be fully prepared before they enter teaching.
4. Professional standards that outline teaching expectations for knowledge skills and dispositions that undergird preparation, professional licensure or registration, professional learning, appraisal, and career development.
5. Preparation and induction grounded in well-defined curriculum content and well-supported clinical training: Teaching and teacher preparation are grounded in thoughtful national or state curriculum guidance, in each case recently revised to reflect 21st-century skills and competencies for students.
6. Teaching as a research-informed and research-engaged profession: Teachers use and conduct research about how to strengthen learning from pre-service preparation throughout their careers. In various jurisdictions, their capacity to engage in practice-based action research is part of admissions and graduation from teacher education, the work of professional learning communities, and a criterion for career advancement.
7. Teaching as a collaborative, not isolated, occupation, where accomplishments are collective, not an individual act of courage. Teachers plan and problem-solve collaboratively and generally have scheduled time to do so. Teachers observe other teachers in action and are observed and mentored so that teacher knowledge and expertise are shared.
8. Teacher development as a continuum: More successful contexts treat teacher professional learning as a continuum toward ever more effective work in support of student learning and, over time, toward the learning of colleagues as well. Collaboration with colleagues is a key aspect of the evaluation process and helps identify teachers for leadership roles.

9. Opportunities for leadership are well developed, tied to formal career ladders (e.g., in Australia, Singapore, and Shanghai) and to organic opportunities to engage in research, mentoring, curriculum leadership, and school improvement activities as part of the teaching role (which are also evident in Canada and Finland).

10. Systems organised to support quality teaching and equity provide an infrastructure of the work of the individuals in the profession. A national or state curriculum, designed by members of the profession and used as a road map rather than a straitjacket, provides a centerpiece for teachers' work and collaborative planning. Stable, reliably funded systems of preparation, mentoring, and professional learning, along with scheduled in-school and professional development time, enable coherent and skilful teaching. Equitable funding and a conscious focus on improving education in traditionally underserved communities aim to ensure that all students will have access to high-quality teaching and learning opportunities.

(Darling-Hammond et al., 2017)

Appendix D
'The Nest' initiative

In relation to issues of **wellbeing**, there is evidence of particular frameworks that are useful for evaluating educational performance and providing targeted improvement support when this is an identified need. The Australian Research Alliance for Children and Youth (ARACY) refer to a wellbeing framework known as 'The Nest.' 'The Nest' framework is for children and young people from birth to 24 years. 'The Nest' conceptualises wellbeing in six interconnected domains:

1. Being loved and feeling safe;
2. Having the material basics;
3. Being healthy, which includes having physical, mental, and emotional health needs met in a timely and preventative way;
4. Learning, where individual learning needs are considered important so that everyone can meet their potential;
5. Participating and contributing, by having a voice and being listened to;
6. Having a positive sense of identity and culture.

'The Nest' may be particularly helpful in managing wellbeing in schools as the framework can be used as a conceptual model for monitoring and tracking students' wellbeing across time; e.g., ARACY has assisted in developing the *Educator Impact Pulse 10 App* to enable educators to monitor students' wellbeing in real time and to guide training needs.

Appendix E

Overview of practices to help promote equity in schools

Drivers of equity	What this means
Anyone can learn	Children are individuals who grow and learn in unique ways. Children are capable of learning and meeting expectations if their needs are supported. Teacher education prepares teachers to think positively about children's capabilities.
Right to early childhood education	Access to early childhood education and care is subsidised by the government and promotes children's holistic growth and development. Learning is in collaboration with parents and incorporates play. The power of play is the foundation of early childhood education and care.
Fair funding and resourcing	School budgets are based on the needs of children and community and follow 'positive discrimination.' Public funds are allocated based on socioeconomic status of parents, immigration demographics, and special education needs. This limits social exclusion and lowers school dropout rates.
Student and teacher wellbeing	School days provide time for breaks from learning and work. School curricula offer a healthy balance between academic seatwork and active engagement through activities in non-academic learning. Play is an important aspect in school.
Health education and care in school	Schools provide children with basic health and dental care, mental health and career counselling, regardless of the characteristics of the population or schools. Annual health checks are part of school life. Schools serve free, healthy, warm lunches.
Balanced curriculum	The curriculum should provide equal opportunities for learning traditional subjects through to interdisciplinary topics, music, arts, physical activity, and play.
Broad-based special needs education	There is a basic assumption that all children have special educational needs. Education is flexible and relies on early intervention and cross-sector collaboration between teachers, health care personnel, and social workers, and is delivered by highly educated teachers.
National youth policy	Social inclusion, opportunities to participate in decision-making over matters of concern, development of individuals' abilities, improvement of living conditions, and access to free-time hobbies and youth work are promoted.

(Adapted from Sahlberg, 2021)

Appendix F

Recommendations for overcoming system failure

Extracted from Bonnor et al. (2021). *Structural Failure: Why Australia keeps falling short of its educational goals*. Sydney: UNSW Gonski Institute, (pp. 21–23).

1. **Agree on the framework.** Having an element of school choice requires smart policies that ensure that benefits are maximised while risks are minimised. But the starting point has to be cross-sectoral and wider community consultation to establish consensus on the purposes and principles that should underpin our schools, as well as the policies needed at the framework level to achieve these. Such a step may seem obvious, but it has never been taken in Australia.
2. **Redesign choice for everyone – or no one.** As it is currently structured, school choice lacks even basic fairness: it can only be accessed by those who can pay, either directly or indirectly, or for those who have what is seen as a 'valuable characteristic.' If choice is to be a priority in Australia, we urgently need to consider the range of options implemented overseas, including restructured school zones, controlled choice, and balloted school entry.
3. **Create meaningful choice.** Choice should be real, such as within and between schools offering innovation and diversity in focus and pedagogy, rather than between schools doing much the same things at different levels in the school social pecking order. Policy and mechanisms need to be revised to maximise the former and minimise the latter. Mechanisms which risk school segregation should be withdrawn or reduced.
4. **Create a level playing field.** A framework which includes a variety of providers should enable each to participate and compete on a fair and comparable basis. The significant inequalities and inconsistencies in the cost, rules, operation, accountabilities, and obligations of Australia's 'competing' schools need to be reduced. Given that a significant proportion of non-governmental schools are funded to the level of similar government schools, a public charter of operation and obligations needs to equally apply to all funded schools.
5. **Recreate the ideals of education as a public good.** The OECD argues that publicly funded schools should be obliged to maintain the 'public good' in

return for that support. They should uphold the basic tenets of fairness and justice in their operations, including non-discrimination among applications for places in the school. Aside from monitoring agreed enrolment practices, a combination of carrot-and-stick approaches, including around funding, may be appropriate.

6. **Create structures which promote and preserve equity.** Properly coordinated funding, strictly on the basis of student need, could have a substantial impact on equity. The bulk of school funding should be on the basis of need, with the process administered by a federal-state-territory authority operating at arm's length from government. Schools with no fees and no discriminators should receive more funding while those which choose to charge fees or apply other discriminators should have their public funding proportionately reduced. There also needs to be a clear focus on equity-related priorities such as inclusion within schools, early childhood education, special education in schools, and wellbeing and health.

7. **Make education systems more demand sensitive.** The OECD argues that the benefits of school choice 'will only materialise in an environment where parents, students, external stakeholders and the local community can participate in the school.' Vital areas impacting teaching and learning, such as curriculum, assessment, reporting, and accountability, need to enable far more school and community participation. This can happen even while some school operations, especially around enrolment and resourcing, are subject to appropriate guidance and, if necessary, regulation.

8. **Maintain a strong state or central education authority.** At first glance, this recommendation seems to contradict the previous, but the focus is on education authorities developing and maintaining a strategic vision and clear guidelines for education and offering valuable feedback to local school networks and individual schools. Major policy development should engage experienced school and community leaders in early design stages, in partnership with system policy leaders. This should also include maintaining standards and agreed levels of accountability, including appropriate levels of monitoring and compliance with an emphasis on sharing good practice.

9. **Monitor and evaluate for equity.** There is a recognised need for new metrics to monitor fairness and inclusion in schools and at the level of the education system. Increased transparency in such analysis and reporting of educational outcomes for equity groups is needed. Australia's most recent Country report from the OECD identifies this as a particular issue: 'Countries can also set ambitious goals for and monitor the progress of disadvantaged students, target additional resources towards disadvantaged students and schools, and reduce the concentration of disadvantaged students in particular schools.' Current annual reporting, on the national assessment program, for example, does not disaggregate data by student SES or even school ICSEA. Many important equity groupings should be examined for trends over time, with routine annual

reporting. Given that equity is a national aspiration, it seems only reasonable to have clear annual reporting against it.

10. **Invest and trust in teachers.** One of the by-products of the current structural failings has been increased downward performance pressure on schools, teachers, and students. Over the last ten years, Australian teachers have been subjected to a raft of initiatives, often focused on accountability and compliance, rather than support and capacity building. An excess of data on schools and students is in contrast to a deficit of data on teachers that has made workforce management and planning difficult; this has occurred as teachers have faced increased workloads and a range of dynamics and controversies that have contributed to low professional esteem. Structural reform of Australian schooling needs to be undertaken in consultation with the profession, with designs aimed at lifting esteem, building professional capacity, and trusting teachers to teach within equitable, well-resourced schools.

References

Bonnor, C., Kidson, P., Piccoli, A., Sahlberg, P., & Wilson, R. (2021). *Structural failure: Why Australia keeps falling short of its educational goals.* UNSW Gonski Institute.

Darling-Hammond, L., Burns, D., Campbell, C., Goodwin, A. L., Hammerness, K., Low, E.-L., McIntyre, A., Sato, M., & Zeichner, K. (2017). *Empowered educators: How high-performing systems shape teaching quality around the world.* John Wiley & Sons.

Hitt, D. H., & Meyers, C. V. (2021). Examining three school systems' actions linked to improving their lowest-performing schools. *Leadership and Policy in Schools.* https://doi.org/10.1080/15700763.2021.1894454

Meyers, C. V., Redding, S., Hitt, D. H., McCauley, C., & Dunn, L. (2017). *Four domains for rapid school improvement: A systems framework.* Center on School Turnaround at WestEd. https://csti.wested.org/resource/four-domains-for- rapid-school-improvement-a-systems-framework/

Sahlberg, P. (2021). *Finnish lessons 3.0: What can the world learn from educational change in Finland?* (3rd ed.). Teachers College Press, Columbia University.

Tang, S. Y. F., & Cheng, M. M. H. (2021). Preparing high quality teacher education graduates in an era of unprecedented uncertainties: The case of Hong Kong. In D. Mayer (Ed.), *Teacher education policy and research: Global perspectives* (pp. 85–100). Springer.

Index